ETIQUETTE
FOR BEGINNERS

The 60+ Basic Rules of Bon Ton for Aspiring Classy Women. Learn How to Be Elegant and How to Behave on Every Occasion to Become an Attractive Lady

Etiquette for Beginners

© Copyright 2021 - All rights reserved.

This document is geared towards providing exact and reliable information in regards to the topic and issue covered. The publication is sold with the idea that the publisher is not required to render accounting, officially permitted, or otherwise, qualified services. If advice is necessary, legal or professional, a practiced individual in the profession should be ordered.

- From a Declaration of Principles which was accepted and approved equally by a Committee of the American Bar Association and a Committee of Publishers and Associations.

In no way is it legal to reproduce, duplicate, or transmit any part of this document in either electronic means or in printed format. Recording of this publication is strictly prohibited and any storage of this document is not allowed unless with written permission from the publisher. All rights reserved.

The information provided herein is stated to be truthful and consistent, in that any liability, in terms of inattention or otherwise, by any usage or abuse of any policies, processes, or directions contained within is the solitary and utter responsibility of the recipient reader. Under no circumstances will any legal responsibility or blame be held against the publisher for any reparation, damages, or monetary loss due to the information herein, either directly or indirectly.

Respective authors own all copyrights not held by the publisher.

The information herein is offered for informational purposes solely, and is universal as so. The presentation of the information is without contract or any type of guarantee assurance.

The trademarks that are used are without any consent, and the publication of the trademark is without permission or backing by the trademark owner. All trademarks and brands within this book are for clarifying purposes only and are the owned by the owners themselves, not affiliated with this document.

Table of Contents

INTRODUCTION	8
CHAPTER 1: UNDERSTANDING ETIQUETTE	12
WHAT IS ETIQUETTE?	12
THE IMPORTANCE OF ETIQUETTE	14
MANNERS IN TODAY'S SOCIETY	15
THE COMMON COURTESIES OF LIFE	16
Traveling Through Your Day	16
From Here to There	17
Social Etiquette	18
Restaurant Etiquette	20
CHAPTER 2: ELEGANCE	22
TIMELINESS	22
MAINTAIN GOOD MANNERS	22
PROFESSIONALISM IN THE WORKPLACE	24
DON'T WASTE TIME	26
MIND YOUR OWN BUSINESS	26
FLAUNTING IS NOT ELEGANT	27
CHAPTER 3: DRESSING ETIQUETTE	28
THE TIRELESS	28
DO NOT BUY IMITATIONS OF FAMOUS BRANDS	30
ELEGANT MEANS THAT YOU KNOW HOW TO CHOOSE	31
Clients	32
Colleagues	32
CHOOSE CLOTHES THAT YOU REALLY LIKE	33
LESS IS MORE	33
Bank	34
Advertising Agency	34
Film Production Company	34
USE BLACK AND WHITE	35
Traditional Business Professional	35
CLEAN SHOES	36
THE RULE OF 3	36
EACH AGE HAS ITS OWN STYLE	37
BEING TOO SEXY NEVER COINCIDES WITH BON TON AND BEING ELEGANT	39

CHAPTER 4: GROOMING ETIQUETTE 40

- KNOW YOUR COLORS 42
  - *Skin Tone* 43
  - *Hair Color* 44
  - *Mixing and Matching Using the Color Wheel* 45
  - *General Tips on Colors* 46
- HAIR 47
- FACE 48
- FRAGRANCE 48
- PAY ATTENTION TO TIMETABLES 49
- MAKE-UP AND NAILS 50
- BATHROOM HABITS 50
- SPORTSWEAR ONLY FOR SPORTS AND AT HOME 52
- LEGGINGS SHOULD BE USED AS SOCKS AND NOT AS PANTS 53
- EMBRACE YOUR SHAPE 53
  - *Athletic* 54
  - *Curvy* 55
  - *Tall* 57
  - *Short* 58
- ACCESSORIES AND HOW TO USE THEM 59
- APPEARANCE MATTERS 60

CHAPTER 5: DINING ETIQUETTE 62

- BE ON TIME 62
- RESPECT YOURSELF 65
- APPROPRIATE ATTIRE 66
- TABLE MANNERS 66
- SAYING "CHEERS" AND WITHOUT NOISY MEETINGS OF GLASSES ... 67
- EDUCATION IS ELEGANT 68
- UTENSILS AND NAPKINS 70
- BE PATIENT 72
- EXCUSING YOURSELF 73
- EMBARRASSING SPOTS 73
- SIT RIGHT 74
- DO NOT PUT YOUR PURSE AND PHONE ON THE TABLE 75
- DO NOT LEAVE TRACES OF LIPSTICK ON THE GLASS 75
- BEWARE OF SPEECHES 76
- THE HOST 77
- DO NOT MAKE UNPLEASANT HAND MOVEMENTS 78
- TOOTH-MOUTH/HAND-FOOT POSITION 78
- WATCH OUT FOR THE GLASS 79
- ATTENTION TO SOUNDS AND MEASURES 80

CHEWING RULES 81
SNEEZING OR COUGHING 82
DO NOT SPEAK WITH A FULL MOUTH 82
LEARN TO RECOGNIZE CUTLERY 83

CHAPTER 6: WORKPLACE ETIQUETTE 86

INTERFACING WITH CO-WORKERS 86
INTERVIEW ETIQUETTE 88
MEETING ETIQUETTE 91
HOW TO MAINTAIN EFFECTIVE OFFICE ETIQUETTES 93
WORK-RELATED ETIQUETTE 97
  Teamwork 98
  How to Treat Your Boss or Supervisors 98
  How to Treat Your Coworkers 98
  Clients and Guests 99
  Considering Others 100
  Being Mannerly 100
  With Time 101
  Avoid Clutter 101
  Keep Your Workspace Clean and Tidy 102

CHAPTER 7: SOCIAL ETIQUETTE 104

SOCIAL SKILLS THAT WILL MAKE YOU A BETTER, SUCCESSFUL PERSON IN LIFE, AND ACHIEVING BUSINESS SUCCESS 104
HOUSE RULES 107
MAKE SURE THAT YOUR HOME IS ALWAYS PRESENTABLE 109
SMILE AND MAKE EVERYONE FEEL WELCOME 111
  Entertaining and Hosting Events Elegantly 112
  What Does It Mean to Be a Host? 112
  Keep the Conversation Going 115
  Saying Goodbye 116
  Dealing with the In-Laws 116
THE PERFECT GUEST 118
GIVE GENEROUSLY 120
USE APPROPRIATE LANGUAGE WITH ALL KINDS OF PEOPLE 123
  Refrain From Negative Comments 123
  Humor or Harassment? 124
NO TO GOSSIP 124
COMPLAINTS 126
PAY PEOPLE COMPLIMENTS 127
ETIQUETTE FOR RESOLVING CONFLICTS 128

CHAPTER 8: COMMUNICATION AND TECHNOLOGY ETIQUETTE 132

SOCIAL MEDIA ETIQUETTE 132
Do 132
Don't 133
LISTEN CAREFULLY TO YOUR INTERLOCUTOR AND LOOK THEM IN THE EYES AS THEY TALKS TO YOU 138
Speaker Phone 138
Taking Personal Calls 138
Cell Phone Ringers and Alerts 139
SPEAK NICELY AND DO NOT USE SWEAR WORDS OR OFFENSIVE TERMS 140
Tone 141
Word Choice 142
Navigating Small Talk 142
WHAT DO I DO IF I SEE SOMEONE LITTERING? 149

CHAPTER 9: BEHAVIOR ETIQUETTE 150

MEETINGS 150
DO NOT BE JEALOUS OR ENVIOUS 151
FRIENDS 153
RESPECT THE LAW 154
RESPECT THE QUEUE 155
DO NOT DISTURB 156
BE MORE FEMININE 157
DISCOURTEOUS COMMENTS 158
BACKHANDED COMPLIMENTS 159
AGE-RELATED QUESTIONS 160
BRAGGERS 160
DELICATELY DEALING WITH DISABILITIES 161
LEARN TO GREET THE RIGHT WAY WHEN YOU MEET SOMEONE 162
POLITE AND KINDNESS 163
Mindful Kindness! 164
Treating Others as We Believe We'd like to Be Treated 164
IT IS ALWAYS GOOD TO BE GRATEFUL! 166
Doing Our Best Because We Care! 168
It's Not Just About You 168
POLITENESS AND COOPERATION 168
AN ATTITUDE OF GRATITUDE! 169
OUR GLASS—HALF-EMPTY OR HALF-FULL? 170

CONCLUSION 174

Etiquette for Beginners

Introduction

Human beings are social animals. We live in communities and interact with each other daily. This connection is so entrenched in us that we have specific terms for people who live outside of society or choose to shut themselves away from it. For the basic survival of the species, it becomes imperative to govern and regulate our social interactions to avoid conflict. After all, punching someone in the face if they offend you is how barroom brawls begin. While it may be emotionally satisfying at that point, it can become a wee bit tedious if you have to do it every day.

This book is dedicated to all women who want to rise their person by improving all the wrong behaviors in public and assuming the right ones. The book is a guide of 60+ basic rules to respect. This book will help women to rediscover the femininity and good manners of the past.

Manners, etiquette, civility, courtesy, and other related terms are simply attempts by the human masses to ensure that our regular interactions don't leave us bloody and bruised. They are codes of behavior that are based on the basic concepts of kindness, consideration, and respect for your fellow human being. These rules become specific so that people feel at ease around you and them. Imagine going to a fancy restaurant and using the dessertspoon to eat soup; it is not a comfortable situation.

Whether you're at work, out with new friends, or mingling at a party, etiquette greases the wheels of social interaction. Knowing what to say and what not to say sets others at ease, and it also minimizes your anxiety when you're in unfamiliar or otherwise-stressful situations. Instead of panicking because you have to go on a business trip with your boss or meet your significant other's parents, etiquette can make you confident about how you'll carry yourself. It serves as a solid foundation that allows you to shine.

Since technology and modern times are much more informal than the days of old, when women wouldn't be caught dead without stockings and men wouldn't dream of leaving the house without a hat, it's tempting to think that we should just do away with the whole idea of etiquette. However, that is just not how people are. We operate by categorizing everything we encounter in the world, including people's behaviors. Practicing good etiquette shows whomever you meet that you care about meeting them and how you present yourself.

This book will teach you how to shine in any situation. Being an adult is hard enough without having to wonder if you did or said the right thing. You'll learn how to make a killer first impression. From introductions and greetings to making conversation with anyone, knowing the etiquette of meeting someone for the first time will seriously cut down on your nerves while setting others at ease.

Familiarizing yourself with basic etiquette will help if you want to be the sort of person who knows how to navigate a formal place setting, comfort a friend who is lost someone, and be a great wedding guest. To look at it another way, all of these are just shortcuts to being your best self. Happy reading.

Etiquette for Beginners

CHAPTER 1:

Understanding Etiquette

What Is Etiquette?

Etiquette, the unpredictable system of decisions that manage grand conduct and our social and business connections, continually develops and changes as society changes. It mirrors our social standards, for the most part, acknowledged moral codes and the principles of different gatherings we have a place with.

It encourages us to show regard, thought to other people, and makes others happy that we are with them. Without legitimate habits and manners, the traditions of pleasant society would soon disappear, and we would act increasingly like creatures and less like individuals. Forcefulness and an "each man for himself" demeanor would start to lead the pack.

On prior occasions, the principles of manners were utilized for 2 purposes: to help individuals remember their own status inside society and strengthen certain limitations on people inside that society. The principles of manners concerning marriage, grieving, and other significant occasions of life to a great extent applied distinctly to the decision classes or the affluent. Laborers and workers, as long as they observed the principles of decorum regarding their relationships with their bosses, were not expected to adhere to formalized guidelines of romance; in general, they based their own "rule" of romance on great habits and good judgment. Throughout the hundreds of years, as society has gotten progressively law-based, decorum has become a magnificent mix of good habits, sound judgment, and decisions of direct that reflect social standards and the principles of our general public all in all as opposed to only one unmistakable gathering inside it. It has less to do with the style existing apart from everything else or who is in force and more to do with not sweating and a moral set of principles.

In this way, practice the best expectations of decorum at home. Be sure to be kind and cordial to your life partner, guardians, and kids, particularly your youngsters, so that they learn to treat others in the best possible way. If they grow up with manners instilled in them, they will think it is simpler to shape enduring connections, be fruitful in their employments, and travel through life as the sort of individuals others appreciate having around. You will also find that behavior turns out to be natural to you instead of a lot of rules, and your own life will be increasingly charming. Individuals react emphatically to the individuals who are pleasant to them and who approach them with deference. Appropriate behavior guides you in how to do this without "missing something" since you just didn't know that something you did or didn't do may be hostile to the next individual.

The Importance of Etiquette

Some people contend that manners are no longer important and that good conduct principles are antiquated and outdated. Notwithstanding, excellent conduct and habits never got out of style. Decorum, similar to all other social practices, advances to coordinate the occasions. Without manners, the citizenry would show excessive fretfulness and disregard for each other, which would prompt affront, unscrupulousness, cheating, street rage, clenched hand battles, and a series of other lamentable episodes.

Etiquette is nothing more than a set of rules of affability and good manners, kindnesses with which we must constantly treat each other. It will consistently matter!

The practical application of the rules of manners and etiquette is known as politeness. It depends on the culture you belong to and can vary from culture to culture. As mentioned in the example about belching, what is acceptable in one culture can be considered eccentric or even rude in another.

Politeness became an art that was cultivated in the coffeehouses of the time. There were rigid rules that defined the language of polite and civil conversation. The concept of civility came into the picture during this time. It referred to social interactions that were steeped in reason and sober debates.

Manners in Today's Society

Today's manners serve a few significant capacities:

- **Etiquette gives individual security.** Realizing how to carry on fittingly in a given circumstance makes you increasingly agreeable.

- **It ensures the sentiments of others.** Legitimate decorum necessitates that you make others agreeable and secure their emotions. You don't bring up their blunders or cause them to notice their errors.

- **It makes correspondence more clear.** Behavior upgrades correspondence by separating hindrances, not raising them.

- **It will improve your status at work.** In any working circumstance, you are seen as progressively competent, increasingly expert, and increasingly astute on the off chance that you know about the best possible set of accepted rules for the work environment.

- **It establishes great first connections.** The initial 5–7 seconds after you meet somebody are vital. Your initial introduction waits in the other individual's brain long after you are no more. If you utilize appropriate decorum, that initial introduction will be a positive one.

The Common Courtesies of Life

The normal civilities of life are the unending little motions we make unknowingly as we travel as the day progressed. As we go to work and wade as the day progressed, we interface with transport drivers, servers, individuals in the city, and innumerable others.

How we associate with these people can influence their day and our own. From approaching a fatigued server concerning grinning at the individual situated opposite us on the transport, the regular kindnesses of life ought to never be overlooked.

Traveling Through Your Day

Traversing the day can be unpleasant for a few of us. On the off chance that you have a bustling calendar, a tiresome day at work, or one of your children is wiped out; you may have a great deal at the forefront of your thoughts that sets you feeling foul. The individuals around you might be feeling similarly as hopeless, yet you don't really need their hopelessness dumped on you, so don't share yours with them. Rather, set aside the effort to be polite and maintain the little courtesies of life, in any event, when you have a feeling that you might want to sock somebody in the nose.

Others will feel much better, and so will you if you keep trying to be polite and share a little smile or joy.

From Here to There

Whether you are strolling, taking a taxi, or utilizing open transportation, you will interface with others while you go from direct A toward point B. Try not to act as you are the main individual on the walkway or street or accept you have the option to proceed in each circumstance. Manners require respect for the safety and others in all cases.

- Pedestrians should never cross-traffic against the traffic light. It hints you are exempt from the laws that apply to everyone else and have no respect for drivers out and about.

- When you are strolling, don't maintain a strategic distance from eye-to-eye connection. Take a gander at others and grin, giving them a concise gesture. It might give them a charming beginning to their day. Try not to gaze; nonetheless, a short look and grin are well disposed and fitting without making the other individual awkward.

- Drivers ought to never utilize their vehicle horn except if it is a crisis and they are attempting to caution somebody to move. At the point when you sound at somebody since you are aggravated on a bustling city road, you are not just troubling that individual; you are irritating many others around you.

- If you will, in general, drive gradually, remain on the correct path. If you are on the left path, you are not exclusively being rude; you are imperiling different drivers who should zigzag all-around ways more to move beyond you.
- When you jump on a means of transport or into a taxi, always welcome the driver and thank the individual when you leave.
- If you see somebody rushing to get the transport, let the transport driver know with the goal that they can pause if conceivable.
- If you and someone else get to a taxi simultaneously, offer to impart the ride to that person. If you are not in a rush and the other party is going the other way, consider offering the individual the taxi and flag down another for yourself.

Social Etiquette

Knowing how to behave in a social setting is key to an elegant appearance. Those with proper social etiquette are able to truly maximize their interactions and create sustainable, long-lasting friendships and relationships. These tips will help you go above and beyond to showcase your elegance in any social situation.

- Keep your engagements. When planning social engagements, ensure that you have the time, stamina, and focus to attend any social gathering before agreeing to attend successfully. If you honestly feel that you will not attend due to an emergency, calling the host or the person who invited you goes much further in others' minds than a text. Canceling plans via text is almost never acceptable, particularly for individuals you don't already know well.

- When you receive an RSVP, always reply. Not replying is not an acceptable way to indicate that you are not attending an event. Always ensure you reply to RSVPs in a timely fashion, whether you plan to attend or not, and be sure to answer honestly; if you're not sure you will be able to attend, indicate this in your reply.
- For gifts, a handwritten thank you note goes miles. A simple verbal thank you shows gratitude, but a handwritten note shows you truly care and value the person who gave the gift.
- When it comes to birthdays, milestones, or rough times in close friends' lives, if you cannot be there in person, a phone call is the best way to show you care. Ensuring they hear your voice to wish them well goes much further in our minds than a simple text or a birthday wish online.

- On friendships and relationships, if you feel you may be overstepping a boundary in any situation, proceed with caution or rethink your approach.

Restaurant Etiquette

- Allow the person closest to the waiter to order first. This helps the staff organize who gets what item and allows everyone to order in a comfortable, sensible fashion.
- Wait until everyone has received their main course to start eating.
- Mind your volume when eating. No one likes to hear chomping, slurping, or any noise coming out of your mouth when there's also food in it. Chew with your mouth closed to minimize any noise and eat slowly.
- At a meal where you are a guest and won't be paying, try to keep your choices at a lower cost rather than ordering the most expensive meal, and stick to items you know you'll be able to finish. Leaving a large quantity of food when you aren't paying can appear insulting to some.
- When at dinner, no matter how large your party is, put your phone away and focus on your companions. If you must send a text or make a call, try your best to do so away from the table to not interrupt the conversation with your discussion.

- After the meal, always leave a tip. Whether the service was top-notch or not, tipping is part of the restaurant world, and you should consider the cost of the tip when deciding to dine out.

Etiquette is key to elegance. Keep those tips in mind to bring elegance to every interaction, every day.

CHAPTER 2:

Elegance

Elegance isn't all about looks. Your behavior and the way you carry yourself are major contributors to how you present yourself to others.

These simple steps will help you present your most elegant self without altering a thing about your appearance.

Timeliness

In any situation, being on time is key. Your arrival in a timely fashion to an interview, party, or event makes a key statement about who you are as a person—organized, thoughtful, and understanding of others' time constraints.

Maintaining timeliness includes adding 20 minutes to your initial commute time if you have difficulty finding parking or get lost.

Maintain Good Manners

Proper manners are key in any situation, but in our modern times, it can be difficult to navigate how exactly to best go about maintaining proper manners.

Some tips for good ways that never go out of style include:

- Keeping your voice/phone/etc. at a healthy volume. Maintaining appropriate volume levels shows poise and elegance.
- Always be sure to introduce yourself to new people as soon as you meet them and introduce any guests you have with you as well. When everyone in a situation has been properly introduced to each other, it creates a more comfortable environment for everyone involved.
- Make an effort to help in a situation in which it seems that another person is struggling, within reason. Take the temperature of the situation before going forward, but when appropriate, help others carry bags, hold doors, and do whatever small tasks need to be done to help another person.
- Respectfully regard the other person in any situation by maintaining comfortable levels of personal space and avoid making the person/people you're with feel trapped by too much interaction or backing them into a corner, either literally or figuratively.
- Never leave a gathering without saying goodbye to the host or the person who invited you. This shows your appreciation for the invite and your appreciation for their company.

Professionalism in the Workplace

Proper workplace etiquette is key when it comes to presenting an elegant appearance. In the workplace, be sure to:

- Adhere to workplace policies regarding punctuality, relationships with co-workers, and general behavior.
- Never enter a room without knocking.
- Ensure that any important communications are written and hand-delivered or e-mailed in a timely fashion. Word of mouth communication is easily forgotten, can make it seem as though your communication isn't important, and can put undue stress on your superiors.
- Respect boundaries of time on the clock vs. off the clock. If your issue isn't an emergency, it can likely wait until a time when you and your co-workers are on the clock to deal with it.
- Minimize phone calls to short, pressing issues rather than constant long-winded calls. This shows respect for the time of the person you're communicating with.
- Avoid being too familiar with new supervisors. Treat every new business relationship with respect.
- Behave respectfully at any after-work function and, in general, avoid having more than 2 drinks, regardless of the behavior of others in the workplace.

They may be comfortable with the possibility of embarrassment, but you should maintain professionalism.

- Always respond to requests or communication given in the morning by the conclusion of the business day. Respond to requests given in the afternoon by the end of the day, if possible, but ensure that all requests from the previous day are taken care of early the following day at the latest.
- Keep your temper in check. Though workplace stressors may seem impossible to quietly deal with at times, maintaining an even attitude and avoiding explosive conflict will benefit you far more than losing your temper or shouting.
- Stay quiet regarding trash talk at work. If someone is speaking ill of someone else to you, there's a good chance they're speaking ill of you to someone else. Disengage yourself from conversations that turn to workplace gossip. You may not want to appear unsympathetic or uncaring, but gossip or trash talk in the workplace rarely leads to anything positive. Keep your head down and do your job as best you can.

Don't Waste Time

Most of us do this daily—and it's truly a waste of potential. Evaluate your life and figure out where you're spending a good portion of your day that's not bringing you any benefit. One of the most common ways to waste time is on social media, scrolling and judging other people's lives, feeling envious of what some people have, or just wasting time looking at things that do not matter in the long run.

Instead of spending an unlimited amount of time watching television or engaging in social media, use that time to better your skills. Whether you want to learn a new language, read a book, or start working on a project you've always wanted to try, there are plenty of things that enhance your overall life and enhance it with elegance.

Not sure whether something is a waste of your time? The best way to determine if it's growing your sense of elegance is to ask yourself this simple question: Is this making me a better version of myself or not? If the answer is no, try to pivot your attention to something that will help you answer yes.

Mind Your Own Business

Okay, this might sound a bit harsh—but it's true! Elegant people do not worry about what everyone else around them is doing because they are more focused on their own lives and trying to make improvements where they can.

Think about the reasons why you might be enticed to watch others—often it's because we are envious of what they are doing or we're trying to make sure we 'stay in the know.' However, acting elegantly means rising above what others are doing and focusing on what you are doing to reach goals or live a more refined life, as mentioned in the previous section.

Flaunting Is Not Elegant

As mentioned earlier, living elegantly isn't about what you have; it's about how you behave and exude confidence. For that reason, an elegant person never needs to flaunt material possessions because to them, they don't define who they are as people.

This is very evident in the comparison of 'old money' and 'new money'—those with old money, such as royals or others of prominence, don't feel the need to show it off and instead keep their wealth a secret from the rest. Those who have new money are often referred to as 'nouveau riche,' which means they like to show others what they have and, in some cases, go so far as to flaunt it.

You can be wealthy or poor and still have elegance—it's about not using your material possessions as a way to define just how wonderful you are to others. Designer labels, jewelry, cars—these things don't tell others who you are, they just show them what you have, and in the scheme of life, it often means nothing.

CHAPTER 3:

Dressing Etiquette

Be careful not to show too much. If you wear an important neckline, you cannot wear a short skirt and vice versa. People make judgments on appearances. It's important to present yourself as a seasoned professional, even if you are new to the working world. Looking professional does not mean that you must lose all sense of your personal style. It is simply about deciding always to remain appropriate and polished. Neatness counts. Never wear overly tight, revealing, wrinkled, ill-fitting clothing to an interview or in your place of work.

The Tireless

Make sure your closet is stocked with essentials that are elegant and timeless, such as a black dress, blazer, heels, white T-shirt, dark skinny jeans, button-down shirt, knee-length skirt, and simple flats.

The dress code has great value in all kinds of functions, parties, offices, businesses, meetings, schools, hospitals, stations, and traveling for both men and women. Etiquette causes individuals to act in a socially dependable manner. Decorum encourages you to gain regard, trust, and gratefulness from others.

There is a colossal contrast between a person's school and expert life. One needs to follow an appropriate clothing standard in the work environment for the ideal effect. It is essential to dress fittingly in the working environment for a never-ending impression. People who dress pitifully are never paid attention to at work.

One must dress according to the event. Abstain from wearing pants, capris, shorts, T-shirts, or sleeveless dresses to work. Follow an expert clothing standard. Ensure you feel great in whatever you wear. Generally, it is not important to wear expensive clothes, but rather to wear something that looks great on you.

Pick proficient hues like dark, blue, earthy colored, dim for legitimate clothing. Splendid hues watch strange incorporates. Light and inconspicuous hues radiate tastefulness and demonstrable skill and look best in workplaces. Ensure your garments are spotless and pressed. One ought never to go pitifully dressed to work. Incline toward wrinkle-free garments.

Females ought not to wear uncovering garments to work. Abstain from wearing outfits that expose quite a bit of your body parts. Wear garments that fit you best. Try not to wear too close or free clothes.

Do Not Buy Imitations of Famous Brands

Make a bad impression with imitations, better an unbranded ten-dollar garment rather than a fraud. The fashion industry is a multi-billion-pound industry with big designers, celebrities, and buyers influencing fashion. However, the final decision on the direction of fashion will ultimately depend on you, the final consumer, who will choose whether to buy into a trend or not.

The interesting thing to note about fashion is that it is essential to develop your sense of style. Fashion should be a means of self-expression and an extension of your personality.

Do not be afraid to experiment with clothes and accessories and be willing to mix and match your items. Fashion should be fun. When dressing up, have a focal point in mind. For women, it could be a big belt or a necklace. Pick one item that will stand out. Be careful not to over-accessorize.

Understand the essential distinction between meeting wear and office wear. Never wear low-neck shirts to work. Pullovers with deep back tabs are a resounding no in the work environment. Dodge straightforward saris. Females who lean toward westerns can decide on light-shaded shirts with dim well-fitted pants. A scarf makes you look rich.

Elegant Means That You Know How to Choose

Did you know that the elegant word comes from the Latin: "*eligere*," which means "to choose"?

Knowing your body, with its strengths and weaknesses, is essential for dressing well. Understanding your strengths is that you can highlight and hide the little flaws you don't like instead. Dressing elegantly doesn't just mean Vera Wang, Versace, etc. It means knowing what looks good on you and is suitable for the occasion. You don't want to turn up for a picnic in a cocktail dress or suit and tie. Clean and ironed clothes add to your appearance. No one likes to look at shabby people except derisively. Remember that any dress that does not have a structured shape is not considered elegant.

It may be true that you shouldn't judge a book by its cover—but it's equally true that the way you look affects what other people think about you and your level of professionalism. For example, suppose you meet with an investment broker because you're considering making a substantial investment. How would it make you feel if the broker were dressed in jeans and sandals and had dirty fingernails? It's likely you'd feel better about the investment if the broker were more suitably dressed. Dressing professionally will also make you feel more capable and boost your self-esteem and self-confidence in a business setting. When considering dressing professionally, you have to ask yourself what message you send. The way you dress is a means of communicating with clients and colleagues. Select each group to learn more about what your appearance conveys to them.

Clients

When you meet clients, the first impression you make is extremely important. You should try to convey a sense of professionalism through your appearance so clients know you're serious about your job and can be trusted to attend to their needs.

Colleagues

A professional appearance and adherence to your company's preferred dress code will let your colleagues know you're there to focus on work. Dressing extravagantly can make people think you are at work to get attention rather than doing your job. Your appearance should be consistent with your professional role. In other words, you should look at the part. You'll inspire confidence in others, who'll be more likely to think you can handle your job well. It makes it more likely you'll command respect and can help you build your reputation and career. Ideas about what constitutes professional dress differ from one industry and organization to another. They also differ based on the position you hold and even based on the country or region you're in. To fit in, you should determine what dress style is acceptable in your organization and for people occupying your position.

Choose Clothes That You Really Like

If you want to revolutionize your wardrobe by starting to buy elegant clothes, always make sure you really like them. Don't buy just because the saleswoman tells you it looks great on you; you have to feel good with everything you wear. However, remember that at the beginning, it can be difficult to change the style. Start putting in one new garment at a time, for example, a nice blazer with a pair of jeans, and start playing with styles and finding your favorites.

Less Is More

Aim for a simple style. Take a cue from French women, always minimal but always the chicest. Although different types of dress are suitable in different scenarios, some general principles for dressing professionally do apply. The first of these is to abide by your organization's dress code—whether this is defined explicitly or implied by the way other employees dress. Your clothes should be appropriate for your organization and suit your position. Different jobs within a single company require different attire. For example, you wouldn't expect a CEO to dress the same way as someone who handles building maintenance. If you examine different work environments, you'll notice different styles of dress. For example, consider how employees typically dress in a bank, an advertising agency, and a film production company. See each type of organization to learn more about its typical dress code.

Bank

If you work in a formal business environment like a bank, you're generally expected to dress formally. Men usually wear conservative suits and ties when meeting with clients or serving customers, and women wear pantsuits or jackets with matching skirts.

Advertising Agency

In an advertising agency, the relevant dress code might depend on the types of clients you typically serve or on the general image that the agency has chosen to portray.

For example, if an advertising agency deals with corporate clients like banks, employees may be expected to mirror the formal dress style of those clients. But suppose an advertising agency wants to project a trendy or more creative image. In that case, employees may wear fashionable designer clothes with a little more flair—including brand-name shirts, slacks, jeans, dresses, and jackets.

Film Production Company

Your position in a film production company would probably dictate what your appropriate attire is. For example, as part of a film crew, it might be acceptable to wear jeans, casual shirts, and even running shoes.

However, if you're responsible for negotiating financial backing with businesspeople, you'd wear far more formal business attire.

Even if your organizational culture allows freedom in how employees dress, overly casual attire may not be appropriate in the workplace. It's often better to play safe and dress conventionally. Another way to help ensure you dress appropriately is to emulate the dress of successful people. Just as a junior lawyer might take cues from the top partners, you can observe and copy other professionals in your organization.

Use Black and White

Black and white compete for the title for the most elegant color. They are 2 colors that also look great together. You can make some fantastic combinations. White can elevate your figure to very high levels, but I recommend it must be an immaculate white, beware of stains. Pastel colors instead give a sense of grace and femininity; learn to use them.

Traditional Business Professional

Always abide by your company's dress code. If you plan to start a new job soon and are uncertain of the dress code before your start date, lean toward the always acceptable business professional attire on day one.

Business, professional attire would consist of a suit, tie, and dress shoes for men. Women have a little more variety. A full suit is one option.

A dress is also a good choice. Just make sure the dress has full closure, meaning no plunging neckline or open back, and is no shorter than 2 inches above the knee. Also, women can choose to wear a blouse, with or without a jacket, and either a skirt or slacks to go along with it and still be considered in line with a business professional dress code. The 2-inch-rule applies to skirts in the same way as it does to dresses.

Clean Shoes

Our shoes say a lot about us. Always remember to check if they are clean and that they are not damaged before leaving the house.

Women should also wear closed-toe pumps, heels, wedges, or flats. This omits sandals, peep-toes, and sling-back shoes of any kind. Today, in most office environments, pumps or heels with a sling-back or peep-toe are typically acceptable but play it safe and take the conservative route until you have more clarity on your news organization's dress code.

The Rule of 3

Do not wear more than 3 colors at the same time. If you want to look elegant, avoid going out like a carnival. Think of your audience: If your clients represent a more traditional organization with a business professional or casual business environment, definitely dress up to what is customary for them. Depending on how you dress for these meetings, it may be seen as a sign of respect (or lack thereof) for your clients. At a minimum, add a blazer to give your casual attire a more professional touch.

Each Age Has Its Own Style

Don't risk looking ridiculous by acting and dressing like a little girl. Each age has its style. The reality of life is that people judge you by the way you are dressed. Being attired in the correct clothing can mean the difference between comfort in a certain situation and feeling out of place. It is a good idea for a lady to carry a shawl/scarf/shrug. You might need to cover your modesty, or the weather might simply change, and you need to cover up.

Gentlemen should have a clean handkerchief in hand, not just for personal use, but it may be handy if a lady should otherwise need it.

Clothing need not be garish; it is courteous to others to avoid attracting attention to yourself. Think of the word 'modest,' which means that your clothes are simple, reasonable, and suit the occasion. Being stylish is about making sure your appearance is smart, elegant and that you are bold enough to create your style. The bottom line is to avoid following fashion or fad slavishly.

The older we get, the less appropriate certain items of clothing become. It is important to be aware of what looks good and keep to those clothing items, rather than following fashion or trying to hold on to youth. For women, miniskirts may be acceptable in their 20s but not as appropriate in their 50s. A skirt just below the knee would seem more appropriate for the latter age bracket.

In temperate regions, the year is divided into seasons: autumn, winter, spring, and summer, and as you know, each day has daytime and night-time. These are all factors that should help you decide how to dress. Usually, each season or time of day has its own easily recognizable fashion to aid a person in choosing what to wear. Avoid the tendency to be carried away by a certain style. Remember to choose carefully. For example, it is inappropriate to be dressed in sequins during the day. Most places have a dress code, which may be written or unwritten.

If an invitation card specifically states a particular dress code, do ensure you follow this. Most schools have a uniform for the children, and the teachers should dress appropriately, even if there is no written dress code. It would be very inappropriate for a female teacher to turn up at school wearing a miniskirt. Different places, e.g., churches, offices, restaurants, etc., have mainly unwritten dress codes.

When in doubt, the safest option would be to wear a plainer dress. It is always better by far to be under-dressed than overdressed. If you are unsure about a ball dress or dinner dress for an event, choose the safer option—the dinner dress. If you are invited to an event and do not specify the dress code, there is nothing wrong with asking the host.

Being Too Sexy Never Coincides with Bon Ton and Being Elegant

Especially after 40, be careful wearing super short, tight dresses with plunging necklines accompanied by super high heels. Essential items for a lady's wardrobe:

- **Little black dress:** A black dress that will suit various occasions.
- **A pair of tailored black trousers:** Straight-leg and flat front.
- **A classic white shirt:** It is wise to invest in at least 3 white shirts.
- **A tea dress:** Midi/knee-length dress; and not clingy.
- **Shoes:** Invest in black medium-height pumps and ballet flats.
- **A navy or black blazer:** Invest in a good quality one that will last for years.
- **Proper bras:** Get properly fitted for a bra. A lot of women are known to wear the wrong size bra. Wearing the right bra can change the way the clothes look on you.
- **Everyday quality classic leather bag:** Start with black before buying other colors.
- **Shawls/scarves:** To keep warm or protect your dignity.

CHAPTER 4:

Grooming Etiquette

The hairstyle is also part of the attire. The hairstyle during the day should be light and simple, without looking that it took several good hours to make it. The makeup during the day will be natural, covering imperfections and giving brightness to the face. The manicure will be as simple as possible not to be distracting. It is recommended to have medium-short and neat nails. The jewelry worn during the day will also be simple and matched with your clothes and accessories. Dresses and blouses should not be very revealing, and the length of the dresses and skirts worn during the day should be knee-length or below the knee.

At formal events or meetings, you should not wear sleeveless dresses or blouses. In this case, the sleeveless outfit should be accompanied by a blazer on top. During the day, no matter how fashionable they are, there will be no glitter or lace clothing.

As for shoes worn during the day should not be high heels (meaning not more than 3 inches tall); the latter is worn exclusively at night. No other type of footwear is allowed for official activities than shoes (e.g., sandals, boots, etc.). In addition, the shoes must be closed-toe shoes. The exposure of the toes is unacceptable in official activities, regardless of the season.

In terms of the handbag, carefully match it with the shoes. The handbag should be big enough to allow carrying an agenda and, possibly, a folder. Women who are dignitaries will never wear a purse during an official activity. Under no circumstances should you see the underwear. Invest in quality underwear and make sure only your lucky partner sees it.

A daily grooming regime should consist of:

- A proper bath or shower.
- Brushing of the teeth and, if necessary, using a mouthwash.
- Moisturizing your skin, especially the face.
- Wearing deodorant and cologne/perfume.
- Wearing clean clothes, especially fresh underwear. Ladies may need to use a panty liner.
- Ensuring that hair is tidy, brushed, or combed.

For ladies, the brows should be well-groomed and shaped. Aim for a natural look; over-plucked arches can create a disconcerting, startled look.

Nails should be clean, shapely, and of equal length. For women, in particular, it is not advisable to wear nail art or nail jewelry. If you are not comfortable with long nails, it is advisable to keep them short and natural-looking.

It is also important to set time aside for yourself. Shave, epilate, or wax the hairs on your legs and armpits, pedicure, manicure, massage, and facial. Ensure that shoes are clean and polished; do not wear shoes that are scuffed, especially heels.

To keep your skin looking healthy and well-nourished, drink plenty of water. Drinking water cleanses the body and re-hydrates the skin. Did you know that drinking at least 2 liters of water daily has been known to burn up calories?

Know Your Colors

Here's the thing, no matter how expensive or stylish the clothes, accessories, hair, and makeup are, they will not suit every one of us. What looks good on your style icon or favorite celebrity may not necessarily work for you. Ladies, you already know that we come in all shapes, sizes, and colors. The most elegant people know how to choose colors (for fashion and styling) based on their skin color, eye color, and even their hair color so that these do not clash.

Therefore, it's not really about picking the Pantone color of the year or going with what's hot on the red carpet or catwalk. Not yet convinced? Check out the benefits of knowing your colors:

- Learning to spot which colors accentuate your best features will make shopping, getting dressed, and going to the salon much, much easier.
- Mismatched colors can make or break a look. Even if the clothes are pretty, they can still make you look dull, matronly, or trying too hard.

- Knowing how to mix and match your best colors can help you create styles that hide your problem areas or make you look slimmer, curvier or more athletic as you like.

Ready to get started? Okay, here we go.

Skin Tone

First up is knowing your skin tone. You can be either warm, cool, or neutral. Here are ways to find out:

- Check the veins on your wrists and arms. If they're more blue or purple, your skin tone is cool. If you have more green than blue veins, you're warm. If it's a mix of blue and green, then you're neutral or olive green.
- Observe the glow of your skin under natural light. If you appear pink, you have a cool undertone. If you appear yellowish or peachy, you have a warm undertone. If you look a bit in between, then you are a neutral or olive undertone.
- Think about the way your skin reacts in the absence of sunscreen. If your skin tends to tan easily, you are warm. If your skin tends to turn red or burn, you are cool, and if your skin burns, then tans, you're olive or neutral.

Warm Skin Tones

- Looks most elegant in the shades of fire and earth like reds, oranges, yellows, and browns.
- Looks best with gold accessories.
- Opt for peach or berry shades for lipsticks and blushes.
- When wearing nude colors, opt for muted or golden undertones.

Cool Skin Tones

- Looks more elegant with sky colors or lower colors of the rainbow, such as greens, blues, and purples.
- Looks best with silver accessories.
- True pink and purplish lipsticks and blushes work best.

Neutral or Olive-Green Skin Tones

- Can wear any color.
- Look better in bronze or gold accessories.

Hair Color

Choosing outfit colors based on hair color is less important than skin tone. However, it is good to know which colors suit your hair color best when choosing a top. Since your blouse will be closest to your hair, it pays to know this bit. For example, if you are a redhead, it does not mean that reds and pinks are total no-nos.

It only means that you would be better off wearing the reds and pinks as bottoms than tops.

- **Brown or black hair:** With white, black, pastels, red, pink, yellow, jeweled blue.
- **Blonde hair:** Earth tones, navy blue, orange, peach, and jeweled green.
- **Red hair:** Browns and earth colors, light greens, light blues, and muted golds.

Mixing and Matching Using the Color Wheel

Get a color wheel from a bookstore or print one off the Internet. Now let's learn about the different color schemes that you can use to mix and match:

- **A complementary color scheme:** 3 colors placed opposite each other on the wheel (e.g., red and green, yellow and purple).
- **Analogous color scheme:** 3 adjacent colors belonging to the same color family, often found in nature together.
- **Triadic color scheme:** 3 colors, evenly spaced out in the color wheel (e.g. yellow, orange, and blue).
- White, black, brown, gray, green, and blue are considered neutral colors that go with almost anything. Generally, you can look elegant with any neutral colors plus a pop of an accent color, which you will base on your skin tone, hair color, and the color wheel.

- Use the color schemes above to effectively color block when you want to use more than the neutral +1 accent color formula. However, this is not to say use all bright shades of the color schemes simultaneously. Elegance means striking a good balance in your use of color. For example, use the analogous color scheme by wearing dark blue jeans, dark purple heels, a white top, and a blue-violet statement necklace.
- Wear dark colors in areas you want to slim down and brighter or lighter colors in areas you want to accentuate. For example, make hips look less wide with darker skirts.
- Wear similar colors of bottoms and shoes to elongate the legs.

General Tips on Colors

Aside from matching the colors with your skin tone, hair color, and knowledge of the color wheel, consider the seasons too. A pop of color during rainy or gloomy weather always looks chic.

- Neutrals are classic elegant pieces that can be worn all over. They are almost as sophisticated as black. Monochromatic dressing a la Audrey Hepburn is always a good idea.
- Never pair black outfits with heavy black eyeliner.
- Deep colors are always more flattering and classier looking than pastels.

- Remember to look at the colors in the patterns of your clothes, too.
- Follow the rule of 3—use a maximum of 3 colors for your entire ensemble, so you do not look like kindergarten artwork.

Hair

Hair looks healthiest when it is clean, smooth, lustrous, and free from dandruff and grease. For ladies, it is advisable to wash your hair at least once a week (depending on your hair type and race) and try to treat dandruff and other issues as soon as you notice them. Stay away from complicated styles that are hard to maintain and try to avoid salons/hairstylists that only follow the styles in fashion. Regular trimming and cutting of hair will enable it to grow healthily.

Avoid bad dye jobs. Color should enhance and compliment your natural tones. Just because a color looks good on someone else does not mean it will suit your skin tone. It is best to have your hair dyed professionally. If you have dyed hair, keep roots at bay and pay for regular maintenance. Try to get your hair done professionally as often as possible. There is a tendency to damage your hair if you do it yourself all the time. The worst is when you apply a relaxer to your hair by yourself.

Be sure your hair is clean and well-groomed. Avoid spiky, wild, trendy styles or unnatural colors. This includes cutting designs in hairlines. Should you find yourself employed in an artistic environment where more flair is acceptable or even appreciated, you can make that decision; however, most offices have explicit policies regarding acceptable.

Face

Women should wash their faces daily and ensure their makeup is understated. They should brush their teeth at least twice daily and should consider carrying breath freshener—for example, for use after lunch or before heading into an important meeting.

Fragrance

Fragrance, also known as perfume, was made only for close encounters. It should be subtle and not overpowering. People are not meant to be able to smell you a mile away before you ever get to them. If the fragrance you want to use is very strong, spray it in the air and walk through it. Spray the scent on your pressure points, behind the ear, the wrist, and inside of the elbow. Heavy or strong fragrances should be used either in the cold months or in the evening. Summer/daytime perfumes should be light and airy. If you wear perfume, aftershave, or deodorant that overwhelms people you meet, you can be sure that's what they'll remember about you. So opt for subtle or neutral scents instead. Also, avoid any kind of unpleasant body odor by bathing or showering every day. Keep in mind that many work environments are scent-free and prohibit the wearing of aftershaves or perfumes to protect employees who may have allergies or perfume sensitivities.

Pay Attention to Timetables

Limit visible piercings to one in each earlobe. The trend of inserting ear gauges may be intriguing to you, but think about whether you will want to have large holes in your ears when you are 30, 40, or 50-years old. They are not professional in appearance and cannot easily be covered. In most work environments, it's best to dress conservatively. So generally, the safest option is to stick with well-fitting, conservative clothes. Avoid loud or garish clothes that will draw people's attention away from your professional role. It's important for men to ensure their suits fit properly and are of good quality. A suit that's scruffy, baggy, out of date, or even too flashy will be perceived as unprofessional. Similarly, a loud tie or shirt is likely to send the wrong message. If you look at your outfit as a whole, you should be able to judge whether all the clothes work together. White socks, for example, won't ever work with a dark suit. Women have more freedom when it comes to dressing, but loud or sloppy clothing is still inappropriate. For example, a shiny, yellow suit is unlikely to convey a suitably professional image. Unless your organization explicitly spells out a dress code, both men and women may have some freedom in choosing what to wear, and a range of different types of attire may be suitably professional.

Make-up and Nails

I see women who fix their make-up on tables in bars and restaurants and in the most unexpected places almost every day. It is not elegant. Make-up and wig are retouched only and exclusively in the Toilet.

Lipstick and lip-gloss are better in neutral or nude shades. Avoid high-shine lip-gloss. Save the red lip and other more dramatic looks for outside of the business environment. Natural-looking nails and nail polish are always appropriate. French and American manicures are acceptable. Avoid designs on nails, including nail art and different colored polish on each finger. Keep fingernail length to a minimum. Extremely long nails are not professional, even with a French manicure. Chipped nails look unkempt and send the wrong message. Keep nail polish remover nearby. A natural nail with no polish is far more appealing than chipped nail polish.

Bathroom Habits

It would be wonderful if everyone respected that cute little poem that you're bound to see in a restroom at some point in your life: "If you sprinkle when you tinkle, please be neat and wipe the seat." Whenever you're finished using a private or public toilet, you should always check to make sure that you haven't left any liquid gifts behind for the next person who uses the toilet.

Also, it would help if you always double-check that you've flushed the toilet when you're done using it. If you happen to come upon a toilet that someone's forgotten to flush, just flush it yourself. Don't find the person and scold her it's one thing to recognize rude behavior, but it's even ruder to point it out to the offender.

If you notice that someone has just come from the bathroom and their zipper is undone, you've got to tell them. Don't shout it across the room, as that will only embarrass them. Instead, take them aside and say it directly: "FYI, your fly is open." They will surely appreciate you pointing this out before it leads to an even more embarrassing situation. Hopefully, if you're ever caught with your fly open, that person or someone else will return the favor.

Along the same lines, if you happen to notice that a girlfriend has spotted through her pants, thanks to her period, she will be eternally grateful if you tell her. Sometimes women's periods sneak up on them, and it's best to find out fast before things get ugly.

Most adults know how to hold their bodily functions in public. However, every once in a while, one slips through. If this happens to you, don't make a big deal out of it. Just say, "Excuse me," and move on.

Sportswear Only for Sports and at Home

Although it seems fashionable to use sportswear for events that are anything but sports, it is not considered elegant at all. Each environment has its style.

Freedom of expression may mean that you can leave the house wearing what you'd like, but the freedom to be well behaved does not. If you don't want to offend people or you're looking to make a good impression on others, you should keep your appearance in mind at all times. Make sure that you put on clothes that are reasonably neat looking. You don't have to go as far as to iron your t-shirts but try to avoid those with holes or stains on them.

If you favor baseball caps, try to wear them in casual situations only, such as when you go to or play in a baseball game. You can probably get away with wearing a baseball hat outside on a sunny day if you've forgotten your sunglasses or you woke up that morning with your bed head.

However, regardless of whether you're having a good hair day, you should always remember that as soon as you go inside a building, you've got to take your hat off. The one time you can get away with wearing something on your head indoors is if you're doing so for religious reasons or it's Easter Sunday, and you're showing off your new bonnet in church.

Leggings Should Be Used As Socks and Not As Pants

Please do not try to look sexy with the help of leggings because they leave no room for imagination. You see everything, absolutely everything. Nothing is less elegant than leggings. Use them only with shirts or dresses that cover your private parts. Women may wear a pantsuit or a suit jacket with a skirt. Slacks and a jacket are usually considered better for business casual wear. Women have more color freedom than men do, but anything understated is still preferred to loud colors. The recommended professional shoe is the classic pump. A professional-looking woman wears a gray pantsuit with subtle white pinstripes, classic black pumps, and a pale pink blouse. To avoid looking sloppy, it can help to organize your existing wardrobe. For example, start by sorting your clothes into categories—casual, professional, and to be discarded or given away. After sorting, you can judge whether you need to purchase any new professional outfits.

Embrace Your Shape

A big part of looking elegant is dressing according to your body shape and body type. Even the most high-end brands look unsightly on people who do not consider the right fit. If it's too tight or too loose, it makes you look short or just plain oddly proportioned; no one will care if it's Gucci, Armani, or Dior. With so many styles and fabric options out there, it is really hard to pick outfits that will look great on you. Therefore, this is where taking stock of your physical attributes and embracing your shape comes in. Generally, 4 body shapes fall into 2 body types. Take a look:

Athletic

- **Characteristics:** Looks slender, toned, and angular with small hips, sharp shoulders, and a broad frame.
- **Body Shape:** Ruler, the body shape of almost all runway models.

Best Looks

- Light fabrics to soften angles (e.g. silk, chiffon, and wool).
- Girly or frilly embellishments, such as ruffles, puffed sleeves, and bows.
- Empire waist, peasants, tops to create the illusion of bust area.
- Flaunt legs in shorts and skirts.
- Peplum skirts give the illusion of wider hips.
- Flared skirts that add more shape.
- Accessorize with statement necklaces and brooches for the illusion of a bigger bust.
- Peep-toed shoes with strappy details emphasize your killer legs.

- A-line cocktail dresses, mermaid gowns with volume, and feminine details.

Avoid

- Manly tops (e.g., military-inspired and button-up shirts).
- Bermuda shorts.

Curvy

- **Characteristics:** Round shoulders with hips and bust flaring out.

Body Shapes

- **Hourglass:** Generally considered as the ideal physique because of the proportion of hips and bust.
- **Pear:** Curves starting from the waist are larger than the shoulder and chest area.
- **Apple:** The shoulder and chest area is wider than the hips.

Best Looks

- Tailored outfits (e.g. with buttons, lapels, and folds).
- Waits-hugging top.
- V-neck tops that draw attention to the bust line and make the torso appear longer.
- **Apple:** capris, A-line or flared skirts, sleek stilettos or nude pumps, off-shoulder tops, and fitted waist.

- **Pear:** dark bottoms, light top, boat collars, scoop or off-shoulder neckline, corseted bodice, sweetheart neckline, pumps, wedges, and boots.
- **Hourglass:** tops that accentuate the waist, pencil cut skirt, fitted tops with high necklines, light-colored dresses.

Avoid

- Adding more curves.
- Empire waist that makes you look pregnant.
- Baggy jeans.

Basic Tips

- When in doubt, go for A-lines, straight-leg trousers, and sheath dresses. They flatter almost all shapes and body types.
- Again, elegant women choose simple classics over trendy ones.
- Try clothes on before you buy them. Alterations cost extra and are only advisable for those who are extra tall or petite.
- Choose clothes that fit you in the here and now. If it's too small or too big, you're probably not going to wear it again.
- Pay attention to the hemline, shoulders, crotch area, pleats and zippers too when you fit.

Elegance is also about comfort. So aside from getting clothes that really fit you well, you also have to consider that the clothes have to be comfortable and pleasing to you above all else. Even if the high heels and blazer combo looks elegant and stylish, you will not carry it well if you feel horrible in it. People will see your pain instead of the elegance you are trying to achieve.

Another important piece of dressing for your body is considering your height. Tall women can wear styles that simply don't work on shorter frames, and vice versa, so when dressing for your size, take your height into consideration and keep these tips in mind.

Tall

- Tall women have more space to rock a bold print, so don't shy away from colorful looks or patterned statement pieces.
- For larger, flowing pieces, add a belt to your natural waist to define your shape and balance your look.
- For pant legs or sleeves that are too short, own that cropped look by cuffing them to create an intentional look.
- Balance your look with accessories that coordinate and tie your look together from head to toe. This creates a more cohesive, pulled-together look.
- Embrace your height by rocking pieces that enhance and emphasize it, like jumpsuits and maxi dresses.
- Wear heels that are only 3 inches tall, maximum.

- For winter weather, embrace long line coats or a knee-length trench to keep warm rather than a more cropped, puffy jacket, as this will create a top-heavy, unflattering look.
- Stick with mid-rise to high-rise jeans and pants, as low-rise will generally not have nearly enough height to cover a longer torso appropriately.
- Avoid anything boxy with heavy, large shoulders or shoulder pads to avoid appearing too top-heavy.
- Check clothing care instructions before washing; shrinkage for a tall girl can ruin a perfect piece.

Short

- Lengthening your look is key for shorter women, so avoid horizontal lines in your clothing patterns.
- Skip shoes with ankle straps. This cuts the leg off at the ankle and makes the legs appear shorter and clumsier.
- Dress up any outfit by adding a pair of nude heels that match your skin tone. This gives the legs a naturally elongated look, whether you're wearing a dress, skirt, or pants.
- Make outfits appear more tailored and refined by tucking in looser tops at the center, letting the rest hang out. This half-tuck helps add structure to an otherwise baggy look.

- To avoid pants looking too long, cuff them just below the ankle.
- Define a loose-fitting dress by adding a belt at the waist.
- Avoid wearing too many pieces at once—an already small frame will be overwhelmed by too much clothing. Choose only key pieces, and avoid too many layers, large, bulky scarves, or more than 2 pieces of jewelry.
- Choose pieces like jackets and blazers that fall at the natural waist or just below the rear. Lengths in between tend to emphasize a short stature.
- Ensure any looser-fitting clothing is balanced with a more form-fitting piece to avoid getting swallowed up by your outfit. For example, a loose-fitting top paired with fitted leggings or pants.
- Avoid large, clunky shoes that will unbalance your look.

Accessories and How to Use Them

Headscarves and scarves should never be worn until they cover the nose. In a business context, accessories and jewelry are worn more by women than by men—but regardless of gender, you should accessorize sparingly. Accessories can say a lot about your attention to detail and imagination, as well as personal taste.

For women, jewelry and hair accessories should be kept subtle and understated. The right choice can complete a particular ensemble, but something large or brash may be distracting and appear unprofessional. It's also important to ensure your accessories and jewelry are of reasonably good quality, or they may nullify your professional image. It's also a good idea to determine your organization's acceptable level of jewelry. For example, it may be considered inappropriate for men to wear earrings, and both men and women may be limited to wearing a single ring on each hand.

You should also consider items such as pens, briefcases, laptop bags, hats, and watches as accessories. These should be of good quality and subtle in style.

Appearance Matters

You may have said that although it's acceptable for women to wear one set of earrings, piercings of any other kind should be hidden or removed during work— especially when meeting with clients. In almost all business contexts, clothing should cover all tattoos.

A further guideline for dressing professionally is to avoid showing too much skin. Many people feel that short skirts, low-riding pants, and low-cut tops don't belong in a professional environment.

Sorry if I sound repetitive, but I want to stress again the importance of wearing clean clothes. It may be common sense, but for those with busy lifestyles, this does take planning. For example, a businessman working late for extended periods might forget to wash or launder his clothes. It's not appropriate to wear stained or dirty clothes to work, and it's advisable to plan ahead so that you always have a spare set of clean clothes. If you want to look and smell professional, never wear the same clothes 2 days in a row. Simply put, make sure your clothes are clean and your shoes are polished.

CHAPTER 5:

Dining Etiquette

Be on Time

Time is the most precious thing we have, one of the few things we cannot buy, and no one should waste it waiting for you. When you have an appointment with someone, always anticipate any setbacks and arrive on time, preferably a little early.

Once you have your reservations, make sure you show up on time. If you don't think you'll be able to get to the restaurant on time, call ahead. Let them know you're running late, and if your arrival doesn't too delay you, the restaurant should be able to honor your reservation. If not, remember it's your fault if you got there late, and you shouldn't expect or demand that the world adjust itself just because you were running behind schedule. If you want to make sure you're never late for a restaurant reservation, set your watch ahead 5 minutes. Alternatively, set the alarm on your computer, PDA, or cell phone to help keep you on track time-wise.

When invited to dine, it is important to plan ahead to arrive on time. Early arrival is encouraged, 5–10 minutes ahead of the scheduled time is preferred. Planning to come early also allows for unforeseeable mishaps, such as getting lost or finding parking.

Take a few deep cleansing breaths before entering an event. Think of the things for which you are grateful. You will walk in centered and will more likely present your best, authentic self. Double-check that you are in good order, buttons buttoned, zippers zipped, hair in place.

A reservation at a restaurant is a promise to show up at a certain time. Therefore, punctuality is paramount; it is not respectful to the proprietors if you waste their time by arriving late. If you have not made a reservation, please ask politely for inclusion. No matter how important this dinner may be, pushy, elitist behavior or attitudes are rude and not acceptable. Once you are seated and receive your menus, try to choose quickly. This does not mean you cannot talk to your companions. Just try to consider that the wait staff has others to serve. Ask about specials and any ingredients of which you are unsure. It is much better to take the time to be sure what is in your meal before receiving it, rather than be disappointed and need to send it back.

If you are a guest, wait for the host to mention what they are ordering. They may want to order a bottle of wine and want to pair it with the food. Additionally, perhaps this meal is meant to be on the *light* side, so you would not want to order too much.

In any case, it is always best to order mid-priced choices. In addition, please thank the host for the invitation.

If you are the host and you want your guest to know he may order anything, mention that there are wonderful first courses that he may wish to try. You may want to comment about the luscious desserts. A conversation is as meaningful as the meal you share. So, as you converse, place your utensils on your plate in an upside-down V shape. Usually, the wait staff recognizes this as a rest in the meal. However, when you are finished with the meal, place your utensils parallel to each other on the right side of the plate. This is the sign for your wait staff to retrieve the setting.

If the event is held at a restaurant, stand in the lobby and wait for the host to arrive. The host will then invite guests to the table. Be sure to stand and greet others. Never sit while shaking hands. If it is not convenient to stand, at least make a gesture that you will rise from your seat.

At business dinners, your guests need to be interspersed with you and your co-workers. Always be sure your business guests are seated near those who invited them. Doing otherwise could cost you an important client or damage a business relationship. The same is true when you are dining with people you manage. Make sure managers and their subordinates are mingling and talking to one another.

Respect Yourself

Nothing is more elegant than a self-confident woman. Moreover, self-confident women really have a high conception of themselves. They know their worth. They know they are unique; they love and appreciate each other with strengths and weaknesses. A woman who knows what she is worth does not allow any comment to demean them.

It goes without saying that when you're eating out at a restaurant, you shouldn't slouch in your seat, take your shoes off, or put your feet up on the table. Can't you just hear Mother Etiquette's voice in your head, asking, "What were you raised in a barn?"?) Those seem like obvious foibles to avoid when dining out. However, other courtesies you need to keep in mind when dining out. One of the best ways to ensure your part as the gracious diner is to make reservations. Not only does this reduce your stress of wondering if the restaurant will be able to seat you, but it also reduces the wait staff's stress of suddenly having your unexpected and large party show up during a busy time at the restaurant.

Eating out in a restaurant is definitely one of life's little joys. You get a night off from cooking, serving, and cleaning up after the meal. Plus, if you plan things properly, you may also get to sample new cuisine or indulge in an old favorite that you can only get when someone else is doing the cooking. Even though you're out of the kitchen, you're not off the hook when it comes to good manners. You still need to act respectfully and responsibly when you're eating in a restaurant—perhaps more so than when enjoying a meal at home or entertaining under your own roof.

Appropriate Attire

Being dressed appropriately when dining out is important. You'd dress differently if you went to a sports bar than you would if you went to a classy steak house. Even though one spot might have numerous televisions broadcasting sports games and scores and the other might have soft music playing in the background with candlelit tables, some basic rules of etiquette should be acknowledged in both types of restaurants.

You may think you know what the appropriate attire is, but the only way you'll know for sure is when you show up (and discover that you're under-dressed) or if you call ahead and ask. When in doubt, consult a dining-out guide ahead of time—either a guidebook or your local newspaper's restaurant section—where you'll often find information about proper attire for certain establishments.

Table Manners

Having impeccable table manners is always a good idea—especially when you're dining out with colleagues and clients—but the truth is your table manners should begin the minute you walk into a restaurant.

For starters, when the host tells you to follow them to your table, do so. Don't rush ahead to where they are gestured you should sit, but instead walk behind them. Once you take your seat, you'll need to remember another whole set of table manners—that is how to have good manners at the table. For starters, you should look at your menu immediately and decide what you're going to order. Not only will this help get your meal underway on time, but it will also help you avoid delaying the wait staff by having to ask them to come back repeatedly.

In addition, even though we live in an age of women's liberation, men should always allow any females in your party to walk first to your table. Men should always bring up the rear. Basic manners are essential in everything we do and a definite must at the table. The basic and most important rule of the table is that we always want everyone to feel comfortable because the essence of good manners is caring for those around you. If we keep this in mind, more than likely, we will make the right decision. So, we would always use all our manners like please, thank you, excuse me and please pass the... Moreover, when someone asks for the salt, give the pepper as well. These 2 travel in pairs.

Saying "Cheers" and Without Noisy Meetings of Glasses

You should simply raise your glass, smiling and saying a wish for which you are toasting. This is right for you to know in case you are invited to a very formal dinner.

Meals must be served at the table on the left side of the host. When you have finished taking food from the left side, you have to move it to the right side. And if you don't have a host, take one and give it to another. In this way, everyone will take all the posts. Generally, liquid foods should be placed to the left of the main position and other foods to the right. Care should be taken to ensure that the position of the food you are trying to eat on the dining table is within reach. If not, then ask the person next to the container to move the container forward. Do not pull the pot over someone else or over the dining table. Nevertheless, if you are within reach, you have to pull yourself up. The rest of the food should be left to the left, and the finished items should be left to the right.

Before picking up everything on your plate as you wish, you have to remember that you can pick up your portion first and then retake it when everyone has taken it.

Education Is Elegant

Never forget to thank and say please. Even if you think people are paid to do what you ask them to do, not for that you don't have to be nice and polite. When a cashier gives you the ticket or helps you or when the waiter brings you or collects a plate, always thank you.

When it comes time to order your food, you should let your guests order first. Try to be as polite as you can when telling the wait staff what you want by saying something like, "May I please start with the salad, and then I'll have the filet mignon? Thank you."

As far as ordering a bottle of wine goes, whoever ordered the wine is the person to whom the wait staff or sommelier (the wine steward) will bring the bottle. Here is what you can expect to happen:

1. The sommelier will present you with a bottle of wine.
2. Don't take it from him. Instead, you should examine the label to confirm that this is indeed the bottle you ordered.
3. The sommelier will open the bottle and hand you the cork.
4. You should check to see that the innermost end of the cork is moist, which is a sign that the wine is still good and has been properly stored.
5. Once you nod your head at the sommelier, he'll pour a small amount into a glass for you to taste.
6. After you've tasted it, you can give him your approval (by nodding your head) that it's OK to pour wine for the other guests at your table.

If you're not satisfied with the wine, you can send it back during this taste test. That's exactly why restaurants do this—they want to ensure your satisfaction with the wine you've purchased. If you feel that the wine has spoiled, tell the sommelier. He should take it back without argument and offer to bring another bottle to replace it. Then you get to go through this tasting ritual again.

You should never be charged for an uncorked bottle of wine that you tasted and sent back because you found it to be unsatisfactory. If you notice a charge for that wine on your bill at the end of the evening, you have every right to dispute the charge.

Utensils and Napkins

An easy rule to follow is to use the utensil that makes the most sense. Say that you are faced with a dish that includes chunky food in a yummy sauce. You may want to use a fork because you want to stab the chunks of food items. However, if you want to taste the sauce, you may want to use your spoon. This is a personal decision, and both choices are correct. Just choose the utensil that makes the most sense for you to use at that time.

If the following course requires the utensil, you just used and has been removed, no problem. You could simply ask for another utensil for this type of meal, or it will automatically be brought out for you.

Once you've ordered and the wait staff has collected your menus, your next move should be to put your napkin in your lap. Do not tuck it into your collar or tie it around your neck, Western-style. Napkins belong in the lap, so be sure to remove them from the table when you sit down. It doesn't matter if it's paper or cloth; the same rule applies to both. It is better to use napkins on the dining table. Spread the napkin on the lap and start eating. If food is stuck in the mouth, you should immediately wipe the face with a napkin or tissue. Food stuck in one's mouth can cause distaste or dislike for other people sitting at the table. If you leave the table in between meals, you have to leave the napkin on the chair. When the meal is over, the napkin should be placed on the left side of the table.

Start your meal by using the utensils the farthest away from your plate, and then work your way in as you work your way through your courses. If you order an item for which there are no utensils already on the table, such as a soup spoon, your wait staff will bring it to you before that course arrives. Make sure you use it for your soup only. You may notice a spoon or fork that's laid out on the top of your plate—those are to be used for dessert and coffee. Your bread plate is to your left, and your drinking glasses are to your right.

You'll find clues about the proper way to use your fork and knife in how your place setting appears. You'll notice that the fork is on the left, so it should be held in your left hand. With your knife on the right, you should hold your knife in your right hand. Don't let your manners slide once your food arrives. You shouldn't eat until everyone else has their food. Always offer to pass the bread, salt, pepper, butter, or other condiments nearest you to your dining companions.

Make sure you chew with your mouth closed, swallow before speaking, and eat at a slow pace. Try to remember to place your utensils down in between bites, and don't forget that napkin in your lap—use it to wipe your mouth if necessary. Speaking of utensils, you should consider following European etiquette to signal the wait staff regarding your meal's progress. If you lay your fork and knifepoint to point (almost like a triangle with no bottom), that says, "I'm still eating." However, if you lay your fork and knife parallel to one another, on the side of the plate, that says, "I'm done, and you can take my plate away."

Be Patient

Do not get nervous if the waiter does not arrive immediately at your table and do not snort, and do not roll your eyes if the lady in front of you in the queue is slow. Elegance knows how to wait calmly. When interacting with the wait staff, be sure you return their greeting when they seat you or come over to introduce themselves. Initiate eye contact, make a note of the person's name, and if you want to go for behavior bonus points, ask him how he's doing today.

It bears repeating that when it comes time to order, you should be as polite as possible. Instead of saying, "I'll take the steak and fries," you might want to say, "May I please have the steak and fries? Thank you." Not only is this a wonderful way to communicate with your wait staff, but also it sets a wonderful example if there are children present. Be sure to thank your server again once the food arrives and all the plates are on the table.

If you need the check-in in a hurry, don't wave your arms madly over your head as you try to get your server's attention. Either tell him/her as soon as you sit down that he/she should bring the check when he brings the food, or politely ask another server to send your waitperson over as soon as possible. Then when he/she gets there, ask for the check.

Excusing Yourself

There may be times during your meal when you need to excuse yourself. It could be to use the bathroom or because you feel that you have a rather large piece of spinach stuck in your teeth. If it's the latter scenario, it's a good thing that you're getting up—you should never fish stray food out of your teeth in front of your fellow diners.

Simply announce to your table that you'd like to excuse yourself to use the restroom, place your napkin on your chair, which signals to the wait staff that you'll be right back, and then push your chair in. If the person you are dining with is getting up, you may want to stand up as the person exits the table. This is especially true for men when a female companion gets up to leave the table.

Embarrassing Spots

From time to time, you may find yourself dealing with embarrassing spots on your clothing, skin, or elsewhere. Ideally, someone else will alert you to this fact, and you can quickly save face by wiping the ketchup off your cheek or changing out of the shirt that has a big stain on it.

A good way to subtly let someone know that she's got something hanging out of her nose is to call her name, then pantomime wiping your own nose. This usually gets the message across loud and clear. After eating it's always a good idea to do a quick of your teeth and face check in a mirror. You want to make sure you don't have anything between your teeth or any remnants of lunch on your face or clothing. If you do, don't take out a toothpick and clean your mouth out. Instead, excuse yourself to the restroom and take a mouthful of water to swish out the stuck food. If that doesn't work, then you can try to pick it out, but only while you're in the privacy of the bathroom.

Sit Right

Learn to sit properly and elegantly. The back must be straight but not attached to the chair. It would be good for a lady not to cross her legs but to arrange them parallel slightly to one side or cross only the ankles as in the famous Cambridge crossing. Before the food arrives, this is not a problem. Once you start eating, keep your elbows off the table. Not only are you crowding someone out of table space (in case you didn't get it, that's rude), you don't want your elbow in someone's soup.

Once you've arrived at your table, you should always defer to the meal's host as to where everyone should sit. If you're the host and this happens to be a business lunch, you should direct people where to sit so that you can take a seat that's in command. If you're dining at a rectangular table, this seat would be at the head of the table. If you're sitting at another shaped table, you should sit in what some called the "gunslinger's seat." This centrally located seat lets you see everyone at your table and the room itself, including the entrance. When you're entertaining clients, you never want to put them in this seat because the room's activity could distract them. Those dining in a mixed company should always let the women in the party sit down first. There's no need to pull out a lady's chair for her and then push it in, but on a date, it's ok if a man want to impress his lady with his chivalry.

Do Not Put Your Purse and Phone on the Table

Never put the phone on the table, neither in the restaurant nor if you are a guest at someone's home. It's rude. The phone must be left in the bag. The etiquette finds that the bag cannot be placed on the table and must be placed on the ground next to the chair if you cannot hang it somewhere.

Do Not Leave Traces of Lipstick on the Glass

Use matte lipsticks because it's very trashy to leave traces of lipstick on the glass. Women, please try to avoid leaving lipstick marks on your glass by blotting your lips before the meal begins. Use a tissue, not your napkin. Speaking of the use of the napkin, use the napkin to dry your mouth before drinking, as food and grease marks on the rim of the glass are unsightly.

If your napkin is a flimsy paper napkin, it isn't necessary to place it on your lap as you may get food on your clothes. When using one, you may put it on the table after blotting your mouth. Just try to conceal any food bits so as not to disturb the other diners. Perhaps you could also place a clean napkin in your lap that will not be used to protect your clothes from spills.

Beware of Speeches

At the table, there is no talk of religion, politics, or money. Avoid these overly sensitive topics, especially when you're at the table and in the presence of someone you don't know well. But if someone introduces one of these topics, do not throw yourself into discussions. Try to change the subject and always respect the opinion of others even if it is different from yours.

These are the things to keep in mind when making plates and bowls. Besides, sipping loudly, eating without washing hands, brushing teeth—these are also indecent. Many people wash their hands on the plate after eating and wipe it off with a cloth after washing their hands. However, this work cannot be done under any circumstances. Our basic instinct at the table is to share, so it follows that conversation is important. Conversations should be pleasant, never argumentative, and should include everyone equally. Humor is usually welcome;

however, degrading jokes are not. Keep the conversation light, talk about the day, current life events, and friends. Avoid discussions others might find displeasing, if not disgusting, like foot fungus. This is also an excellent opportunity to introduce children to the rule of not interrupting others. We want a peaceful setting in which to enjoy the meal and the company of others. The pace of consuming food slows as we share pleasant conversations as if we are "savoring the flavor." If you find that you tend to rush through your meal, perhaps savoring the flavor could be your new motto. Others should not feel obliged to rush through their meal to catch up with you. Be considerate, slow it down, and enjoy the company and the meal you share.

- Please.
- No ethnic humor, disgusting topics, politics, or religion.
- No discussions of bodily functions.

The host

If you are invited to someone's house for lunch or dinner, the bon ton involves bringing a gift. The host will always give the start of the eating. If we have both a host and a hostess, then the hostess will be the one giving the cue for starting, which is done either through a gesture or verbally. In the case of drinking, the gesture belongs to the male host. If no couples are present at the table, the host will start, regardless of sex, both for food and drinks. If it is a business meal and there is no host, wait until each person is served before you start. The host gestures for the meal to end. After making sure all guests have finished eating, she will get up from the table first. However, if a guest of honor is present at the table, they will have to be the first signaling the leaving, at least half an hour after all meal courses were served. It is impolite that some guests leave before the guest of honor, especially when all guests are seated at a single table.

Do Not Make Unpleasant Hand Movements

Don't crack your fingers, don't put them in your nose, and don't scratch yourself in public. A great oldie but goodie rule is the one about our elbows. We all know this one: elbows should be close to our sides, not flapping about or placed on the table. However, did you know that we may place our elbows on the table under certain circumstances? Absolutely! The one exception is when you are having a conversation with a tablemate. If you place your utensils down on the plate, you may lean forward with an elbow on the table. This body language conveys that you are interested in what they are saying.

Tooth-Mouth/Hand-Foot Position

When we can't pick up food with a spoon, we try to push it with our fingers, which weakens our own personality in front of others. So this issue should be avoided as much as possible.

Again, some people start knocking on the table to get the food stuck in their teeth. This is very embarrassing. So when removing the stuck food, you must cover your face with your hand and take it out with the other hand. Sneezing is a very familiar habit to us, but it is a very offensive behavior in front of everyone else at the dinner table.

Do not swallow large amounts of food in your mouth at all times, but do not remove the bones or thorns directly from the mouth when eating with a spoon.

Watch Out for the Glass

Never hold the glass by the cup, always by the stem or base. Now that the wine glass is in your hand look at the wine. Tip your glass, holding it away from you. You are looking for visual clues of quality; one is clarity. A wine that appears murky will taste as such and vice versa.

Each varietal has its own hue. Look for that color. Time will change the color or hue of a wine. For example, older, high-quality red wines will pick up a browner, almost opaque tone. White wines also gain color as they age; it is natural for some wines to turn warm amber. If a light-colored wine, such as a Pino Gris, turns amber. However, it is not good. Learn your varietals and the corresponding colors. All it takes is time, which means more tasting and talking to people; that is why many of us love wine tasting.

No, you are not ready to taste the wine yet—more looking. You are now looking for legs on your glass. Swirl the wine counterclockwise if you are right-handed. As you gaze through the glass, you will see legs or tears streaming down the sides. Supposedly, this tells you the sugar content of the wine, which indicates alcohol and richness. Some sources swear by this, and some discount it. I believe more legs indicate a fuller mouthfeel. In addition, swirling incorporates more air into the wine and opens the bouquet.

Attention to Sounds and Measures

Don't make noises when you eat or drink. Body language is so fundamental in everything we do because our body language speaks for us. It indicates how we feel about ourselves, the people around us, and our environment. So please, be attentive to the way you sit at the table.

So, what is the proper body language at the table? We do not recline, rock, or tip in your chair. Instead, we sit up straight but relaxed and not stiff. Alternately, don't sit overly stiff as it is possible to dribble food all over the front of us. We lean forward slightly from our *hips* when taking a bite—bringing the food to our mouth, not our mouth to our food.

Returning to the subject of tipping and rocking in our chairs, I have a very good friend who is quite stout. Recently, he joined us for a nice brunch, and because he is quite large, he bent one of my chairs by merely tipping back. I was so embarrassed for him, but thankfully, he did not notice the chair. It would have ruined our enjoyable afternoon. What kind of grooming would you imagine would be allowed at the table? Trick question! There is no grooming at the table, including picking your teeth, cleaning your nails, combing your hair, and applying makeup. Even though some restaurants may provide toothpicks—at a counter by the door— (I wish it weren't so), these are not for use at the table or use in the presence of others. Using a toothpick has the same visual effect as flossing at the table.

Finally, our last reminder speaks to those whose heads are always so cold that wearing their hats to the table seems appropriate. Don't. Just please remember what your first-grade teacher probably told you every day. Don't wear your hats indoors, especially at the table.

Chewing Rules

If it is seen that the person sitting next to you is chewing loudly while eating, then the desire to eat should not exist anymore. Not only that but also many people may lose their appetite for this word of chewing gum. For this reason, eating loudly at the dinner table is a sign of manners. You can get rid of this word by playing with your mouth closed. You may be eating with great satisfaction, but the person sitting next to you may not be able to eat at the sound of your chewing. This sound is caused by opening and closing the mouth while chewing.

Many of us love to eat fish bones or meat bones. Playing at home is another matter. Nevertheless, at a party or restaurant, it is quite a sight to behold. This practice should be avoided even in front of small children—because they will take it for granted and imitate it.

Sneezing or Coughing

The habit of sneezing or coughing while sitting at the table facing the food is very offensive behavior. Therefore, if you sneeze or cough, you have to turn your face to the other side. In that case, the face must be covered with a handkerchief or hand.

Do Not Speak With a Full Mouth

The dining table is our small hangout. It can be seen that the whole family is getting together after the day's work and maybe they are meeting at the dinner table. How the entire day went, what happened during the dinner is completed through these stories. In addition, that's why at this time you must be careful not to talk about food in your mouth. You have to answer or talk after finishing the mouth food. Otherwise, spilled food can ruin the pleasant atmosphere of the dining table.

After eating, wash your hands in a specific place and wipe your hands with a towel or tissue. When you get up from the dining table, tell the person next to you to get up from the table. This will show your politeness.

Learn to Recognize Cutlery

The position of the knife-spoon and plate indicates who is well-mannered or fashionable. One of the things you need to know to present yourself uniquely on the dining table is the use of knives and spoons. Knife-spoon, placing a corner between the plates means you are resting between meals. Putting it as a plus sign means your plate is ready to eat, and the waiter will serve the food as well. Horizontally parallel or side-by-side, it means that the food is very much liked. Placing it vertically parallel or vertically side by side means the end of eating. The waiter can take your plate. Knife-spooning one inside the other, making a corner by inserting the knife inside the fork-spoon means you have finished eating but did not like the food at all.

There are also different rules on how to hold a knife and a spoon.

- The knife will be in the right hand and the fork in the left hand in the continental system. The right-hand knife should be held close to the plate. Moreover, with the fork on the left hand, you have to put the food in your mouth. At this time, the spoon should be rotated towards the plate.
- However, in the American method, the fork in the left hand must be eaten with the right hand. When taking a break between meals, keep the sharp side of the knife facing the plate in a continental manner. The fork should be turned upside down and placed

horizontally on top of the knife, so that the knife and fork are cross-shaped. The position of the spoon and the knife in the American method is a little different. Here, the fork part of the spoon (not inverted) should be facing upwards, and the knife's sharp edge should be facing towards itself. The position of the knife and spoon will be angular.

Etiquette for Beginners

CHAPTER 6:

Workplace Etiquette

Interfacing with Co-Workers

It is basic for a person to act in a socially worthy manner. Manners cause a person to appear as something else and stand separated from the group. One should be not kidding and somewhat reasonable in the work environment. An individual can't carry on a similar path in the office as they do at home. Individuals who need etiquette are never paid attention to by their kindred laborers.

An individual in solitude thinks that it's hard to make due in the working environment. One should be a decent, cooperative person to make their imprint in the working environment. They need to interface with their kindred laborers and offer plans to reach better arrangements. Representatives must work as one for quicker and compelling outcomes. Keeping up sound associations with individual laborers is fundamental as they invest their greatest energy in the working environment.

- **Respect your laborers.** This is part of the company or organization. Without this, people will never grow, or we can say they will never succeed in their careers. Therefore, colleagues and employees must be respected.

- **Be cheerful with everyone and greet everyone with a smile**. It is a terrible habit to make faces at others. Figure out how to be a little more changing. Things don't generally go in your direction.
- **Help your partners in the manner you can.** Never give them any off-base proposals. You will like your activity more off chance that you have a companion in the work environment.
- **Be polite with your colleague and co-workers.** If anybody yells on, you never yell back at them. Try not to do what others do. You won't become little if you state "sorry."
- **Too much friendship at the workplace is harmful.** Being state forward at your workplace. The other individual may exploit your liberal disposition.
- **Never go overboard.** It pays to be very relaxed in the work environment.
- **Abstain from favoring one side in the work environment.** Try not to request individual favors from any of your co-workers. Never ask anyone to do your grocery shopping for you or pick up your child from school. It is unprofessional.
- **Abstain from being impolite to anybody.** No one can tell when you may require any of your kindred specialists. Never lash out at others under tension.

Never interfere with your associate's work. It is a bad habit to open other individuals' envelopes or browse through individual specialists' messages. Regard your associate's security. Try not to peep into any other individual's workspaces. Thump before entering your supervisor's lodge.

Interview Etiquette

Behavior refers to great habits that help change a woman into an elegant woman. An individual must act well openly to pick up regard and gratefulness from others. It is basic to carry on in a socially worthy manner.

An interview is nothing more than an association between the company and the potential representative. The company tries to make a judgment about the person in different positions for a job. An individual must do well in an interview to be a piece of their fantasy work. Interview etiquette refers to codes of conduct an individual must follow some instructions while appearing for interviews. Some interviews etiquettes help to attract an interviewer:

- While showing up for telephonic meetings, ensure you have your resume before moving to a calm spot and keep a pen & paper helpful to write down a location or other vital subtleties.
- An individual must be available at the meeting scene before time. Leave your home a little in advance and allow a margin for traffic jams, vehicle issues, route

worries, and other unavoidable conditions. Check the route well in advance to maintain a strategic distance from unforeseen events.

- If you don't have your car, book a taxi or ask your companion or relative to drop you off directly at the gate. Abstain from passing by an open vehicle on that day.

- Be specific about your appearance. Follow the expert clothing standard for a never-ending early introduction. Wear something that looks great on you. Arrange a light-toned shirt with an admirably fitted, muted-toned pair of pants. Make sure that your shoes are clean and don't make clamor. Hair should be perfectly brushed and have a soft smell. It is fundamental to smell pleasant.

- Enter the interviewer's lodge with certainty. Welcome them with a comforting grin. A strong handshake says that an individual is certain, forceful, and ready to take difficulties. Try not to offer to shake hands if the questioner is a female. Try not to sit down, except if you have been advised to do so.

- Make an eye-to-eye connection with the questioner. Abstain from looking to a great extent.

- Be fair with the interviewer. Recall a solitary untruth prompts a few different falsehoods. Maintain a strategic distance from counterfeit stories. It may land you in a difficult situation later.

- Take care of your pitch and tone. Be considerate but firm.
- Stay quiet. Abstain from being anxious during interviews. Recollect nobody will balance you until death if you don't clear the meeting. There is consistently another opportunity.
- One must sit straight for the ideal effect. Abstain from tinkering with pen and paper. It is critical to have the correct disposition, as it encourages you to stand separated from the group.
- Keep your PDA in the quiet mode while going to interviews. PDA ringing during interviews is an offense.
- Chewing gum during the interview is silly.
- Do not overlay your resume; rather, keep it in an appropriate organizer. Convey all other significant records you may require during the meeting. Keep an identification size photo convenient.
- Slangs and jokes must not be utilized in interviews.
- Avoid breaking messes with the interviewer.
- Once you are finished with the interview, remember to thank the interviewer.

Meeting Etiquette

Behavior alludes to great habits required by a person to discover a spot in public. It is significant for a person to act suitably in broad daylight to procure regard and appreciation. One must figure out how to keep up the respectability of the workplace. It is imperative to regard one's association to anticipate the equivalent consequently. Nobody could ever pay attention to you if you don't carry on well in the work environment. Release us through some gathering behavior in detail:

- Try to discover what the meeting is about. Representatives should do all the basics before going to meetings to ensure the greatest cooperation on their part. The plan notes ahead of time.
- Never go to meetings without a notebook and pen. Essentially, a person with memory may not remember everything discussed at the meeting. A notepad helps to jot significant focuses for future reference.
- Always keep your mobile phone in silent or vibrating mode. Mobile phones ringing in gatherings and classes are viewed as impolite and amateurish. This may affront others sitting in a similar room and break the pace of the gathering.
- Do not answer calls during gatherings, except in a crisis. It is a bad habit to do likewise.

- Superiors must make a plan before each meeting. The plan must flow among all workers to prepare in advance for them to get ready ahead of time. Gatherings ought not to be directed only for them. Make sure you do not deviate from the key points. Keep the gatherings short.
- Never be late for meetings. Going late for a gathering is not something normal for an expert.
- Be a decent audience. Tune in to what others need to state. Trust that your turn will talk.
- Sit any place you discover a spot. Try not to run to a great extent.
- Do not go into the meeting room once the meeting has just started. It upsets others.
- Avoid taking your cups of espresso or tea to meeting rooms except if and until prompted by bosses.
- Fiddling with a pen or scratch pad is one of the significant interruptions in meetings. One must think and remain alert. Be a mindful audience. Try not to yawn regardless of whether you discover the meeting exhausting.
- The one leading the meeting must talk noisy and clear. It is fundamental to deal with the pitch and tone.
- Meetings should be intelligent and permit workers to think of their recommendations and significant

input. An inquiry answer round must be kept toward the end for workers to clear their questions.
- Once the meeting is finished, minutes of the gathering must be arranged and coursed over all divisions for them to make an important move.
- Use Whiteboards, projectors, diagrams, pointers, slides for better clarity.
- Do not convert the meeting room into a battlefield. Talk graciously and do regard your partners.

How to Maintain Effective Office Etiquettes

In a business situation, it's essential to stay proficient regardless of the organization's chance of a fun and relaxed environment. Convincing office etiquettes go far, although there might be requirements and laws regarding worker procedures. The key factor the staff must do is to be easily efficient.

Professionalism will gather respect and present chiefs and kindred associates that you're not kidding about your career and can take every necessary action. There are positive things that show great office etiquette. Knowing these key tips offer with surviving in an office situation some help to a worker. Next, avoid easy transactions with regard to your personal life during business hours. Talking to collaborators about your activities or your kids in a relaxed discussion is fine. Be that as it can, don't stay too much in these conversations or present cozy details of your personal life. Another great office etiquette routine is to differentiate your work email from your personal email. However, revealing well-disposed emails between collaborators must be done utilizing your personal email address. At any time, an IT person or a director can access your email, and you will need to make sure you are using yours for its proposed cause. It is great to grin and giggle; however, feeling that things are not going well in the workplace may indicate that you cannot handle certain situations. Whether it is a high-end office or a fast-food restaurant, etiquette standards are crucial regardless of nature. Representative pleasure will be expanded by taking after these policies. They will similarly produce spot or the office of business an exceptional workplace. Here are a couple of normal etiquette considerations:

- **Understand that time is important to organizations:** do not allow being late for work. You may not be the person who offers indulgences every day. Being late implies that you have little commitment to the association and the job.
- **Email etiquette:** avoid piling up emails in light of the fact that you will get more every day. Indeed, and acknowledgment of receipt is sufficient. Try not to click Reply to all emails; it is not necessary.

- **Telephone manners:** Answer your phone after 3 rings maximum. Casual, business or any type of call must have the ability to achieve the target within 3 minutes. Beyond 3 minutes can be proportional to misuse of the phone. Use appropriate communications strategies. Utilize your personal cellular phone for personal communication.
- **Personal visits:** visits should be after work hours or at lunchtime. It is unjustifiable for the company for you to engage in social chit-chat during working hours. If it must occur, allow it to be by agreement and in extremely sensitive, life-threatening situations. Your family and friends should know that you must respect your work time.
- **Internet use:** this equipment may be handled incorrectly. Addictions to discussions on social networks; however, can cause work objectives to be overlooked.

  Make your internet use remarkably careful. Internet misuse has caused numerous people to lose their jobs. In several nations, they check your online action by checking your users to see what kind of person you are and searching for you on Google.

- **Dress issues:** Your job will let you know what type of clothes to use. It is easy for you to come to work dressed in overalls and be the general manager of the advertising office. Most organizations allow Fridays to be relaxed clothing wear. When the particular use of a uniform is established, guarantee its use.

- **Work with a purpose:** The absence of a purpose leads to a lack of goals and objectives; "Are the things you did today related to your desires and work objectives?", "What did you do all day?" You must know when to make things personal. As a guideline of confidence, you cannot give up on your dreams, regardless of how critical they may seem. Your work goals first, and then take a look at other things.

- **Budgetary integrity in the task environment:** You may not be an accountant or the worker responsible for the money, but from time, you have the opportunity to handle money to a budget item. Stop having views on other people's income. You can be progressive with your income.

- **Relationships:** Relationships make the organization. In any business, workers will need to have a meaningful working relationship. When you work with someone, you tend to get to know them better as the days go by, they might take care of some of your problems, but they are not your partner.

- **Have a calm perception in the work environment:** Avoid clogging your brain with personal plans. Your mind should be focused on what you have to finish and your goals for the day. Refrain from consuming intoxicating substances during working hours, and after working hours, you can do whatever you need to do with your objectives.

Work-Related Etiquette

There is a social element in most offices, so observe the protocol and remember that your behavior will affect your future. Once people see you misbehave at work, it is difficult to get that visual out of their minds. This is why it is essential to get off on the right foot from the beginning. However, if you've already made some mistakes, people tend to forget over time, but you'll need to be patient and maintain good manners, even when people make comments about your old ways. Most working people spend more waking hours at the office than at home with their family, so it's worth establishing and maintaining solid business relationships, no matter how difficult it might be. You should develop trust in each other or the work will be more difficult. Remember, you are all working towards the same goal. If you have a problem with one of your coworkers, take it to HR but never talk it out in front of other people. This takes hard work, but it can pay off in the future, making the difference between career success and failure.

Teamwork

Companies typically expect their employees to be good team workers and do their jobs to better the whole. This means that you must accept your position in the overall order of the corporation. Remember that every job is important, or the company wouldn't spend money on salaries, benefits, and training. All employees, regardless of their position, should feel free to greet each other in passing. Don't be afraid to say good morning or good afternoon in the hallway.

How to Treat Your Boss or Supervisors

The truth is you should treat all people with the same amount of respect just because they're people and you're educated and classy. Of course, it is a whole different thing to deal with a manager than with a coworker that's on your level, professionally speaking.

How to Treat Your Coworkers

If you are new at your job, take some time to observe how everyone acts. Test the waters and avoid commenting on topics that you don't fully understand. Once you have established yourself as a congenial team player, go ahead and let your personality shine through. Do your best to cause a good first impression, as they are very difficult to change. You should learn a few things about your coworkers, such as their names and titles, company acronyms that apply to your job, and task and reporting responsibilities. If someone asks for volunteers to assist on a project, be the one to step up and offer help. When the moment comes, and you need others' assistance, they will be more likely to cooperate with you. People will appreciate your hard work and commitment but avoid patting yourself on the back too often, as you might come across as a bragger. How to maintain a good relationship with your coworkers.

- Never repeat anything negative.
- Avoid participating in office gossip.
- When handling cash, have another coworker present.
- Never call a coworker "sweetie," "honey," or any other term of endearment, even in jest. It may come across as sexual harassment.
- Never take credit for a coworker's idea or work.
- Always praise your coworkers for a job well done.
- If you want something, remember to say "Please" and "Thank you."
- If you carpool with coworkers, set rules for the trip on the way to and from work.
- Show respect for your coworkers during business hours and when you're out of work.

Clients and Guests

You are likely to find yourself in the position of interacting with clients or guests in your workplace. Smile, introduce yourself while looking at them directly, and ask if and how you can help them. Offer something to make them more comfortable while they wait. This can be a seat, coffee or water, a magazine, or even food. At that moment, you are the company's face, be sure to make a good impression.

Considering Others

Being considerate of others involves simply considering how your words or actions affect others and adjusting your behavior accordingly.

For instance, a secretary works for 2 partners. One of the partners, who's under a lot of work pressure, sarcastically asks, "Are you ever going to be done with that?" In this case, the partner should have considered the secretary's feelings—and the fact that the secretary might be under pressure to complete other work.

Being Mannerly

Good manners are as important within working environments as they are outside of them. Saying "please" and "thank you" goes a long way, although there's more to it than that. For example, a salesperson who keeps a client sitting in a waiting room while attending to a personal call isn't displaying very good manners.

Manners are just as important in today's fast-paced age as they ever were. Most individuals never mean to offend others, but bad manners can ruin work relationships and create unhealthy work environments. To be professional and avoid damaging working relationships, you should endeavor to understand and respect others' needs. You also need to meet their expectations about what constitutes appropriate behavior.

Business etiquette refers to the standards or guidelines that determine what constitutes good manners and professional behavior in the workplace. The basic rules of business etiquette might not be spelled out explicitly, but they determine what the people around you expect and consider appropriate, given your position in an organization.

With Time

Expectations about how businesspeople should dress and behave change with the times as prevailing social norms and conditions change.

For example, it used to be considered much too familiar to use people's first names in a business correspondence unless you knew those people extremely well. But it's now fairly common practice to use people's first names after you've met them only once or twice.

Avoid Clutter

A second important guideline is to avoid clutter. Clutter includes all unnecessary items taking up space on desk or table surfaces or even on the floor. For example, it might include piles of papers and books, coffee mugs, assorted stationery items, and personal ornaments.

Every few months, Nikki adds another framed photo of her young daughter to her desk. There's now little room left for work-related papers or files.

It's appropriate for Nikki to include some photos of her daughter in her workspace. However, she should choose just one or 2 recent inappropriate frames to prevent her workspace from becoming too cluttered.

Keep Your Workspace Clean and Tidy

Paul is highly conscientious and often works through his lunch breaks. Normally, he takes just 10 minutes to eat a sandwich and have some coffee at his desk. With being so busy, he has failed to notice several coffee stains on his desk and folders—and these aren't likely to make a good impression on visiting clients.

Instead, Paul should consider having his lunch away from his desk, even if this involves taking just a short break from his work.

CHAPTER 7:

Social Etiquette

Social Skills That Will Make You a Better, Successful Person in Life, and Achieving Business Success

Why are a few more lucrative than others at the beginning and maintaining relationships or beginning new business walks? Imperative parts are assumed by unique personality traits suffering from a comprehensive selection of outside components in determining who gets to become successful in life. Social factors like reputation, prior experience, capability.

It is about connection, whilst invention seems to have limited our capacity for direct person-to-person contact. Whatever the case may be, we must inspect the interpersonal skills that could be paramount to becoming successful in all life groups.

1. **Social network**: Grasp a social network or make one. Cultural expertise exercises need bunches for expansion and engendering. Visibility to data is less stressful through systems; more individuals with more data types influence, trust, and power, and more people imply more information. A written report by the American

Academy of supervision in 2000 demonstrated that business persons having social skills like referrals, standing, systems, and personal connections will most likely get to monetary money from shareholders than those without these characteristics.

2. **Take the project and be deliberate**: Successful people are conferred, inventive and flexible. They take the initiative to be social, exhibit the ability to study, and exhibit significant technological skills. Assume the responsibility to enhance your delicate skills by having a picture of your communication skills and reinforcing your ability to manage stress, whether self-incited or forced.

3. **Mutual respect**: Treat others as you expected that could be handled. Grow your energy by featuring mutual respect, opposition, ability to give and take comments. Show certifiable acknowledgment and thankfulness when something fantastic happens to your own kindred. An acclamation of certifiable evidence is an indication of self-sentencing. Finding time to recommend success with an alternative person is contagious and is free.

4. **Ask questions and speak less:** The endowment of-crevice isn't like a matter of course, the understanding function of those who seem normally motivated workers. These types of men are not reliable with people. The ability to ask different questions is just a

social understanding that may improve your relationship with people.

5. **Look:** Have you ever been in a conversation with someone who is looking at their cell phone or simply looking elsewhere? A lady was accepted through the assembly procedure; she just oversaw attention-to-contact with her planned manager twice; however, all for a vital conference in her spot as of late.

6. **Be observant, pay attention to details**: Many of us are experiencing peaceful franticness. Only the extremely observant folks can see what issues in accomplices or your link's change in outer appearance and non-verbal communication. This could provide additional knowledge on the best approach to the required problem, which could be an essential turning point for this relationship.

Understanding and mastering these skills will help you be more productive. Spend more time talking less and being more watchful. The right inquiries and ask people can unify along with you. Everything is considered; we're able to checkout fulfillment in 3 or 2 manners. A couple of people learn about societal partialities or company traits or eating tastes and abhorrence of family members and allies around us.

House rules

Daily, you're surrounded by people who know you best—but does that mean there's no element of manners or etiquette to be used?

Every home is different, where the customs, traditions, and cultures also vary. When you visit someone's home, you get a good idea about what that person is like—from the physical environment to how you are greeted when you arrive.

If you're a guest in someone's home, it's continuously expected that you follow whatever traditions or customs are established in that home. For example, if you arrive at your co-worker's house and their family removes shoes when coming inside, you will need to do the same to be mindful of his space and show proper grace and respect.

Respect and consideration also go for adults living together in a home. While you both share a single space, creating an environment of thoughtfulness and courtesy goes a long way toward establishing a healthy and calm life at home. How do you act gracefully even if no one's watching?

- **Give each other alone time.** Whether you each have separate hobbies or you just need some quiet time after a long day of work, it's considerate to give each other time to spend alone. Though you might think that 'alone time' means your partner wants to get away from you, it's actually good for the relationship to develop interests that don't include the other. This allows each of you to build trust and remain individuals, strengthening the overall bond of a relationship.

- **Always respect privacy.** Privacy is a big deal for relationships—it might be difficult to consider that your partner doesn't tell you everything. To provide the utmost respect, don't go through personal journals or diaries, mail, or text messages.
- **Respect each other at home and in public.** The way you present yourself and your partner shows others how they may receive you. It's not proper to air your dirty laundry in front of others—especially if they are intimate in nature. When in public, refrain from insulting or putting one another down—aside from being deeply humiliating, it gives others a bad impression of your relationship.

Maintaining proper manners and etiquette in the home is even more important if there are children present. It's in-home where children learn the foundation of respect and manners— they often imitate what they see and hear, so it's vital that you and the other adults in the home set a good example.

Make Sure That Your Home Is Always Presentable

Don't be unprepared in case unexpected visitors come to you. The house reflects a lot of our person. However, don't obsess about looking for perfection that doesn't exist. The house can never always be perfectly in place precisely because you live in it. I am referring to avoiding accumulating, for example, garbage, dishes that have been dirty for days, in short, things that make the house, and therefore you, look dirty. Speaking of unexpected visits, they are not considered elegant in etiquette. Even if you think you are making a nice surprise by suddenly introducing yourself to a loved one, you always think that you could catch them in a bad moment and embarrass them, so always try to warn them in advance.

There will probably be others living in your college dorm room, apartment, or home at any point in your life. Whether you willingly moved in together or you needed to share the space to make it more cost-effective, learning how to live with others and stay respectful and graceful does take a bit of work—even if you love the person cohabitating with you, such as a spouse or child!

If you're in the market for roommates, you must consider your own lifestyle before selecting someone to live with you. What happens when you like to be in bed by 9 p.m., but your roommate is a night owl and wants friends over every weekend? Alternatively, what if you're very tidy by nature, but your roommate likes to be messier?

Understanding your own personality and what you're willing to deal with will help you make a positive choice for a roommate and will allow you to have a more positive experience. Of course, you're not always going to have a say in who lives in your space—such as whether you're assigned a roommate in a college dorm or you have to live with others in a military setting. In this case, establishing proper manners and boundaries is a good way to create a comfortable living environment. No matter what your living situation is, 3 things you need to remember:

- Commitment.
- Communication.
- Compromise.

Once you've signed a contract or a lease, you need to be committed to following the house rules if you live with someone or establishing a good living environment for your partner. Check in with each other periodically to make sure that each of you is doing your fair share and working as a team (or group) to keep the living space clean and welcoming.

Communication is key in any relationship, whether it's related to roommates or partners living together. Every person living under the same roof has a responsibility to do what they can to make the home a comfortable and safe place—which is why communication is very helpful. What happens when you do your part by cleaning up after cooking or taking out the trash every evening, but your roommate or partner leaves dirty clothes all over the apartment or forgets to pay the rent even though it is their responsibility?

Frequent meetings or chats help make sure that issues don't go unresolved for a long period. Doing so breeds resentment and eventually anger—so create regular check-ins with each other to ensure that all issues are taken care of on time.

Compromise is another helpful tool in any personal relationship. It helps the overall mood of the house, and it can be a realistic option for dealing with some of the most unpleasant tasks—such as you taking out the trash while the roommate empties the dishwasher each evening. While you might not love doing every single one of your tasks, compromise is more about what you can do to help.

Living together takes an element of respect and trust in both of your parts. Common manners go a long way to creating an environment that benefits everyone living under the same roof.

Smile and Make Everyone Feel Welcome

When you meet someone you know or introduce you to someone you don't know, always give them your best smile. You will convey serenity, and everyone will always be happy to meet you. When someone new joins the group, perhaps your friend's new girlfriend, immediately make her feel comfortable with her and share the conversation so she can relax and gain confidence. You will leave a beautiful impression of yourself on her. She will remember that you will be the one who helped her integrate into the group. You have to put everyone at ease with you; they need to relax and feel good in your presence, obviously not to the point that they can afford excessive confidence. If you are not very confident with friends and relatives, avoid touching a person without their permission.

Entertaining and Hosting Events Elegantly

when one thinks of etiquette, the first thing that typically comes to mind is hosting parties or events inside and outside of the home. As you can see throughout this book, etiquette and manners play a role in nearly every aspect of our lives—from how to properly communicate with your co-worker over the Internet to what to say (or not to say!) to a pregnant woman.

Socializing has been a part of life from the earliest civilizations! The moment someone enters your home, there is a dynamic in play: the role of host and guest. Even if someone wants to come over to watch the big game or to have a simple conversation over a cup of coffee, there are always expectations of both the host and the guest.

What Does It Mean to Be a Host?

When you invite people into your home, you want to give your guests a sense of welcoming and warmth. It might be an overwhelming thought to host a number of people over to your home for a celebration, especially when it includes aspects such as:

- Serving food or beverages.
- Make sure all your guests are welcomed and introduced to each other.
- Setting up the area for the event, whether it's the dining table or outdoor space.

Thinking about all the aspects of a party could feel like a lot to you, but a good thing to remember is that being a gracious host takes all the same manners and etiquette that you exhibit in other areas of your life. The planning process and learning how to multitask during the event take a little more care as a host.

As with all things, practice makes perfect. Your very first dinner party might not go as smoothly as you would have hoped, but when things don't go as planned, you're able to consider them for the next event. Did you find yourself too rushed and stressed the day of the event, setting up the party or dinner space? Next time, start the day before and get the table set earlier in the day so you can focus on other aspects of the event. Planning also means creating a welcoming environment in your space—the group of people you invite has a major impact on the type of party you will have! Fun and interesting guests will turn any event into something amusing and lighthearted, while grumpy and judgmental people will create an element of stress and anxiety for all invited.

So, what makes a good host? Here are some of the most important aspects of proper party planning, which offers plenty of courtesy to guests and helps keep things a little less stressful for you:

- **Provide details when sending out the invitation.** Your guests might not like to show up to your event and be completely in the dark, let them know what type of event you're hosting so they can come prepared. If you're hosting a swanky dinner, a printed invitation—which is more formal in style—will highlight the event is a little more important than a football party on the weekend.
- **Try to have everything ready before guests arrive**. While there are always last-minute details to fix, ensure that all the major features are completed well before the guests arrive. A good rule of thumb is to be done and dressed for the event no less than 15 minutes before the party begins.
- **Set the tone.** If you welcome your guests to your home like a chicken with your head chopped off, it sets the tone for the entire space, and your guests will begin to feel as if they are in your way or a nuisance. Getting ready for the event early also allows you to take a deep breath, have a glass of wine and welcome your guests into a calm and relaxing atmosphere.

Hosting with proper etiquette also means you're the one who will direct the event from start to finish. What does this mean? You'll announce when cocktails are over, and dinner begins, as well as when dinner is over. Allow your guests to begin eating after 4 or 5 people have been served, so the food does not get cold. A graceful way to begin any dinner party or social event is to start with a toast.

The thought of giving a toast might send shivers down your spine, but it doesn't need to be anything too verbose or complicated. Simply thank your guests for taking the time to come to your home and wish them health and happiness before they dine on your meal. If you're celebrating a special event, a few words regarding why you've gathered is also a great addition to a toast.

Keep the Conversation Going

One of the most difficult aspects of hosting is keeping your guests mingling and interacting if they don't know each other. As a host, it's proper etiquette to ensure everyone feels welcomed and a part of the festivities! Just as you will pay close attention to whether your guests are getting enough food or beverages, you'll also want to watch and see that some of your guests are feeling left out of conversations.

Small talk, which we went over in an earlier chapter, is one of the foundations of cocktail parties. Mingling and introducing one another is typical—so there is less for you to do as a host when it comes to keeping the conversation light and friendly.

Once the dinner starts, your task will be to keep the lulls in conversation at a minimum—no one likes to eat dinner in silence while at a party! Inevitably, topics of conversation might come up that create a debate amongst guests, and while some groups can handle a livelier conversation, it's up to you as a host to keep any topics from getting out of hand, especially if there is a mixed crowd at the table, consisting of old friends and guests who are new to each other.

Saying Goodbye

Do you find it awkward to tell guests to pack up and leave? At the end of the event, it will be time for guests to leave, and you don't want to drag it out. Here are some simple tips you can do to wind the party down and let guests know the party is ending:

- Stop serving food or beverages, such as after-dinner coffee or cocktails.
- Turn the music off and begin cleaning up the trash around the room.
- Tell your guests in a friendly tone that you're exhausted and have an early start in the morning.

Dealing with the In-Laws

Does the word 'in-laws' conjure up frightening memories, or do you get along well with your partner's parents? After marriage, you gain a set of parents—though they aren't exactly strangers, they have their own set of customs and traditions that you need to be aware of when interacting with them. As more cultures are blended through marriage in the coming years, it will be more common than not to be blending a household with religious and cultural traditions.

As is the case with dealing with any person, there are a few basic points of etiquette to implement into your interactions:

- **Be tolerant and willing to accept differences.** One of the best ways to keep the peace between families is to avoid interfering or inserting your opinion on everything. Different families have various ways of doing things, so to keep the family peace and your life stress-free, accept the differences and be tolerant even if you don't understand them.

- **Do not look for hidden meanings.** It could be difficult to hear what you deem a flippant remark from your mother-in-law, but there's also a good possibility she meant nothing by it. If you look for double-meanings in everything your in-laws say, it could lead to an abundance of resentment and create fractures in the relationship—especially if you go to your spouse and want them to pick a side. The best way to manage is to take what they say at face value and let it go if there truly is a misunderstanding, confront it quickly and with grace so that it doesn't continue over time.

- **Do not hold on to grudges.** It's not good for you, and it's not good for your relationship—especially because it's your partner's parents and putting them in the middle is never a good idea. You have 2 options—you can talk to your in-laws if it's worth fixing, or you can try to move on and give yourself peace of mind.

The perfect guest

In someone else's house, do not allow yourself to open doors or drawers and the fridge. Don't venture to explore the house. Only the host can take you if he wants to do a tour. Just as there are tips and guidelines for being a proper host, there is an equal number of suggestions and actions for guests. Manners are important no matter where you are—but when you're invited to someone's space, you must show courtesy and respect. Here are some of the best ways you can show etiquette after you've been invited to a party:

- **Be there on time.** Plan your arrival at the event between 5 and 15 minutes after the start time, but never show up earlier than the time provided on the invitation. This cuts into the time for the host and isn't something they should need to accommodate. If you think you'll be more than 15 minutes late, it's respectful to let the host know so they can move on with the festivities or wait for you.
- **Do not be on your phone.** It's simply poor etiquette to have your phone go off while you're in a dinner with others. Turn your ringer off and don't

answer any calls while you're at the table—if you see that you need to make a call, be sure to excuse yourself from the table and make the call in a different room.

- **Be gracious and considerate.** Your host has taken a lot of time and effort to create a dinner party or special event—not to mention the costs included for food and beverages. Always be gracious to the host and thank them for the invitation—it's also kind for you to compliment them on the food choices or the atmosphere!

- **Be an active guest.** Whether that means conversing with some new people or playing a silly game with the rest of the guests, do your best to stay a part of the action. Not only does it make the other guests feel inclusive, but also it helps alleviate some extra stress for your host if they think you're not having a good time.

Once you've seen some visible clues that the party is winding down, please take it as the opportunity not to wear out your welcome. Proper etiquette highlights that guests can easily stay an hour after the meal to enjoy a coffee or cocktails, and then guests should start leaving unless they are invited to stay longer. On your way out the door, be sure to thank the host once again for a pleasant dinner or party—if they're not at the door, then go and look for them to say a personal goodbye.

Does the idea of providing a gift to the host seem confusing? Depending on the reason for the party, a gift might be proper etiquettes—such as if it's a housewarming or a special occasion. If you're invited to a dinner party and don't see each other often, a hostess gift is always welcome and appreciated. The hostess gift doesn't need to be anything too involved—a bouquet of flowers, something small for the house (like a candle), or a nice bottle of wine are all lovely tokens of thanks and are sure to be well received by the host.

Read your invitations and abide by the rules. Make sure you know who is invited to the party. Do not assume that your family is welcome to attend the company holiday party. Companies usually have budgets set aside at the beginning of the fiscal year for employee parties and teambuilding events. An open invitation to spouses, partners, and children can quickly add up and go over set budgets. Some companies see the party as not only a holiday celebration but as a time to reinforce company values and connections. When adding spouses, partners, and children, employees tend to be distracted and are less likely to socialize with their colleagues.

Give Generously

Elegant women always have a big heart; greed and attachment do not exist in them. They love to help others in many ways. A good way to help others is not just as a charity, but also by giving away your time and attention. Sometimes people just need a shoulder to cry on.

It feels really great to nail it when giving a gift. Finding that perfect whatever and watching someone get all giddy when they open it is the best! However, it's not always easy. Giving a good gift doesn't require spending a lot of money. It's more about thinking about the recipient and what they like, what they value, and the memories you have together. A cheap snow globe you know they loved but lost as a kid that you managed to dig up online for $3 can be worth more to that person than 100 times that amount of money.

If you're giving a gift for a wedding, you can certainly still go the thoughtful-but-inexpensive route, but it had better be thoughtful for both people in the couple. There is no hard-and-fast rule about wedding gifts, but typically, people expect you to spend $50–$75 if they're a distant relative or coworker, $75–$100 for regular friends and relatives, and $100–$150 for close friends and relatives. Buying from the couple's registry or giving a check are fail-safe options. Remember that while paying to travel to your friend's wedding is incredibly kind of you, it's because you love them and want to be present to support them; it does not count as a gift for the bride and groom.

Office-oriented gift-giving is a little different. You by no means have to give your boss a gift for the holidays or her birthday, but if you really like her, you might genuinely want to. If you're unsure what to do, ask a coworker what the office culture is. There might be rules against gift-giving, or your team might like to pitch in for group gifts. If you end up buying one on your own, small and thoughtful are the ways to go. A nice bag of coffee or a tote bag with their favorite team's logo is a pretty safe choice. On the other hand, Gag gifts can go wrong, especially if they are opened in front of others. Avoid them!

If you want to buy gifts for your coworkers, small and thoughtful are again the key. When you're buying for your whole office or team, you can give the gifts at the office party, but if you're only buying for one or 2 close friends, give them the gifts privately, so no one's feelings get hurt. If you're on the receiving end of a gift, no matter who it is from or if you love it or hate it, be delighted that someone thought of you and gave you something. Your reaction shouldn't be to the gift itself so much as the lovely, thoughtful gesture of someone giving you a gift.

A good rule of thumb is always to send a thank you if you receive a gift. A thank-you email is sufficient if you had a small birthday get-together where people gave you fun little gifts. If the party was large and people traveled or got dressed up to go, a handwritten note is best. On the other hand, if you were touched by a gift—or action—a handwritten note shows a level of personal gratitude that email just can't match.

No matter the format, a thank-you note should be personalized. "Thank you for the gift" doesn't really cut it. You should thank them for the specific gift, even if you didn't much care for it. It's the thought that counts, right? You can mention where you placed it in your house or how much you enjoyed using it. If that gift was money, you can thank them for their generosity and even mention what you might spend it on. The letter can be short and sweet, but more never hurts if you have a lot to say.

One non-gift-related event that calls for a thank-you note is a job interview. You can send an email or a handwritten note, depending on the vibe you get from the company. Thank whoever interviewed you for their time and mention that you look forward to *hearing* from them, but don't get pushy or presumptive and say you look forward to *working* with them.

Use Appropriate Language with All Kinds of People

People love their fellowmen, someone they can identify with, so avoid having an overly sophisticated language with people with a very low cultural level because you would make them uncomfortable. Conversely, try not to be unprepared when talking to educated people who use refined language.

Refrain From Negative Comments

It's important to refrain from making negative or disparaging comments about your employer, coworkers, superiors, or clients in any public forum. For example, if your manager refuses to give you a day off, don't post offensive or threatening status updates about this on your social media profile. If your manager or colleagues find those comments, it could compromise your reputation and your career.

Humor or Harassment?

It is undoubtedly desirable to work in a place you feel comfortable. It's even better when you can consider it fun and enjoyable to go to work! However, having fun should not come at the expense of coworkers, creating an uncomfortable workplace for others.

It is hard to determine when a joke or a comment crosses the line and becomes an insult or a form of harassment. This is mostly because a lot of it has to do with perception. In addition, while some people are more sensitive to comments than others, you can limit the likelihood that you will be on the wrong end of a harassment complaint by censoring your comments and actions at work.

Simply put, nationality refers to citizenship. If you are interested in asking someone about their ancestry, the more appropriate question to ask may be, "what is your ethnicity?" Even then, the topic is sensitive and should be approached with caution.

No to Gossip

Remember that it is not for elegant women to speak badly of absentees. You know very little about the life of others, it is easy to judge the choices of others, but you don't know anything of the real reason why others do a certain thing. Much better to talk about a whole hour than to start telling, "What you heard about." Be that person where gossip dies. Others will appreciate you much more and remember that those who gossip about others in their absence will do the same thing with you when you are absent, so do not give much confidence to these types of people.

To begin with, maintain a tactical distance in the normal office gossip constantly. It's important not to urge or add to remain without moving gossip. Doing as such will affect your fame with administrators and colleagues. There'll dependably be persons in any office that'll begin the chat or add to it. That you don't need to be one of those individuals.

I am sure you can come up with a name or 2. It may be the person who wears the loud cologne and a comb-over hairstyle. On the other hand, it may be the person who uses football analogies for every conversation they participate in.

Whomever it may be, try your best to resist sharing your views or comments with others in the office, no matter how funny you think they are. Now, if I were to ask, "Who do you absolutely despise at work?"

Hopefully, the answer is not that easy to find. And if it is, I hope for your sake that it isn't someone you work closely with on a day-to-day basis, such as your manager or direct report. Whatever your answer is, I would urge you not to share any negative views you may have about them with others at work.

Bonding with coworkers over gossip or the dislike of other individuals in the office is juvenile and unprofessional. It creates an unhealthy working environment. Predicating or encouraging this type of behavior is not helpful to anyone. You do not have to be friends with everyone you work with, but making disparaging comments about someone or sharing your ill feelings about a coworker to others in the office creates bad energy.

Use your head. If you are up for a promotion but have a reputation for gossiping, it will not go over well with HR or upper management. Gossiping makes you appear immature and possibly untrustworthy. It may give your leaders reason to question your ability, if given authority, to maintain confidentiality about sensitive company information or employee matters.

Complaints

Occasionally, we may be discontent with a level of service or when sold a defective product. We might complain about a rude member of staff, an undercooked meal, a misplaced order, etc. When we complain, it is usually because our expectations have not been met or satisfied.

Ideally, we should complain to right a wrong, which may benefit others and allow the company or business the opportunity to correct the problem.

If you have to complain, try to stay calm and avoid yelling, shouting, cussing, or screaming. If you do, you are unlikely to get any result, and the people involved will most likely be put off by your behavior.

There are keys to complaining: Know who to complain to—It is usually best to speak to someone in authority. However, you should always try to resolve the issue with the person you have a problem with.

Pay People Compliments

A great way to build social skills is with compliments. Every human being wants to feel appreciated; we all love praise. Complimenting people can be tricky because, first and foremost, you want to come across as sincere. The last thing you want is to be perceived as a flatterer. Therefore, be conscious of 'over complimenting.'

When paying compliments, make statements that you know to be true and stay with the specifics. Try complimenting someone on their achievements, *e.g.,* if they have just completed a task successfully. When paying compliments, make sure that you look the person in the eyes and smile. This will make you come across as sincere. There are polite and decent ways to say things. For example, saying "You look good in that dress" is more complementary than "I like how that dress looks on you." An even more complementary way would be to say, "You make that dress look good."

A genuine compliment will make the recipient feel good about you, earning you more points in the social scene. However, please, only offer genuine compliments.

Lastly, avoid double-edged compliments. A double-edged compliment is when you give a compliment with one hand and take it away with the other. For example, "Wow, well done, I heard you got that job; did your dad put in a word for you?".

Recipients should acknowledge a compliment with a "thank you" and a smile. If someone says you look good in an outfit, a simple "thank you" will suffice; there is no need to give the history of where you bought the dress, how much you paid for the shirt, or that the shoes were a bargain. A well-paid compliment will almost certainly leave the recipient happier and with a warm feeling.

Etiquette for Resolving Conflicts

When you're part of a conflict, no matter who's to blame, you should always try to resolve it. You can resolve conflicts by following 4 rules of etiquette: be the first to make a move, choose the right time to approach the other person, be conciliatory, and take responsibility for how you've behaved.

When you have a conflict with someone, it's always good to be the first to attempt to resolve it. In a conflict situation, the other person might actively avoid you due to feeling uncomfortable and not knowing how to deal with the conflict. In this case, it's best to confront the conflict by approaching the person directly.

This person will likely appreciate you making the first move and so will be more open to finding a resolution. However, it's important to choose the right time to address a conflict. You can approach the other person privately and as soon as possible after the conflict occurs to organize a sit-down meeting.

See each guideline for approaching someone for more information about it.

- **Approach in private:** You can approach the other person in private to avoid embarrassment. For example, you could approach the person quietly in their office or when they are alone in a common area.
- **Approach as soon as possible:** It's easy to avoid conflict and pretend it's not happening, but this won't solve anything. You need to approach the person as soon as the conflict arises or as soon as you become aware of it. It's best to deal with a conflict as early as possible to stop it from getting any worse.
- **Organize a meeting:** When you approach the other person, you should explain that you think there's a conflict between the 2 of you and politely ask if it would be possible to discuss it in a meeting. Don't start by accusing the other person of wrongdoing.

Try to meet at a calm time of day that suits you both. For example, a meeting after lunch might be more constructive than one first thing in the morning when you're still trying to organize the day.

When you meet with a person to discuss a conflict, make sure you're conciliatory, and avoid showing any anger. Heated discussions can make a conflict worse. If you act calmly, it will encourage the other person to respond calmly too. Remaining conciliatory will help both parties stay objective and logical. A final guideline for resolving conflict is that you should always take some of the responsibility. Conflicts are very rarely caused just by one party.

You should apologize for any of your actions that you think may have exacerbated the conflict. This doesn't mean you're taking responsibility for the whole conflict; you're just taking responsibility for your part in it.

For example, if you think you may have reacted unnecessarily to something the other person said, you can admit this and apologize for it. This may encourage the other person to apologize in return and help you overcome the conflict.

CHAPTER 8:

Communication and Technology Etiquette

Social Media Etiquette

Social media is the place where your work life and your social life will most likely collide. Think of how much fun it is to Internet-stalk that random person you met at the coffee shop, in whom you have no real interest. So imagine how keen employers are to check up on their prospective and current employees!

If you want to have a polished online presence that represents the real you without jeopardizing jobs or friendships, these dos and don'ts can help you get there.

Do

- Stay positive. Words of encouragement, celebrations of achievements—those are things people like to see.
- Be selective in whom you connect with and what you post.
- Keep it interesting by posting about lots of topics instead of just your own day-to-day.
- Think about the long-term effects and the public nature of social media before you post.

Don't

- Lie or misrepresent who you are.
- Troll or get involved in online flame wars. They just aren't worth your time, and they can make you look really bad.
- Post personal stuff on your company's accounts or feeds.
- Share sensationalized or false news. Do your due diligence!

Of course, thinking about who is on the receiving end of your text should play a part in what you type. Texting with a friend means you can be as casual and emoji-laden as you want, but it still pays to give your messages some thought. You want to say what you're trying to say instead of having to rapid-fire 5 more messages explaining what you really meant.

As for texting friends while you are at work, try to keep that to a minimum. Nothing irritates bosses more than finding out that all that feverish typing is actually someone figuring out where they're going to dinner.

There are a few things to remember about chatting at work that will not only make you look good but also keep you out of hot water. First, follow your office culture's lead. If everyone is chatting, go for it. If barely anyone uses it, only chat with those who message you first, especially higher up the corporate ladder than you. Some people are bothered by the chat.

Second, before you start a chat, think about what you need to say. Chats aren't for hour-long conversations to decide how to proceed with a project. They're for quick things like confirming your boss wants to review the presentation at 11 a.m. or figuring out who is picking up the coffee and baked goods for the client meeting. Depending on the people you work with, they also might be up for joking around and seeing if anyone wants to grab a quick afternoon kombucha down the street.

As the use of the internet continues to expand into every aspect of people's lives, from emailing and social networking to scheduling job interviews and doctor's appointments, many of us have become complacent, formed bad habits, and tossed proper etiquette aside. This is unfortunate and may create problems if we don't learn and apply a few basic rules. Internet etiquette is essential in a civilized work environment or personal relationship. Remember, you can know everything about a person just by going through their social media. Of course, people try to show the best version of themselves on social media, and that's okay. I see them as platforms to show the best moments of your life or other special things you enjoy with your friends and loved ones, be careful with who you accept and give access to your pictures and information.

- **Keep messages and posts brief:** Most people use the internet to save time, so honor that and keep messages as brief as possible. Unless, of course, you are talking to friends or people you have more connection with. If you have more to say, try breaking it up into smaller topics. This will force you to be more organized and enable the reader to digest the information orderly.

- **Do not shout:** Avoid using all caps in any emails or posts. Some people think that keeping the caps lock button on for the entire message will make it easier to read, while it actually does the opposite. It is not only more difficult to read, but it also comes across as if you were shouting, which is perceived as rude.

- **Protect personal information:** Since everything you post on the Internet is out there for everyone to look at, avoid adding personal information. This includes your address, phone number, credit or debit card number, social security number, driver's license, or passport information. You don't want this information to be easily accessible to identity thieves or predators.

- **Obey copyright laws:** Never copy someone else's work and post it as your own. It is against copyright law because it is considered stealing. It is always good to ask for permission before quoting anyone, but that isn't always possible. If you want to quote someone, keep the quote short, cite the source, and add a link to the complete written work. Before clicking the "send," it is always good to reread anything you type before clicking the "send" button.

Step away for a few minutes and come back to it with fresh eyes if you have time. If not, check your spelling, grammar, and tone of the message one last time before sending it. If it is late at night and you are exhausted, it is probably best to wait until the following day. You can save most messages and posts in draft mode.

- **Help others:** If someone appears to be new to the internet, offer your assistance. Share information on proper etiquette, send them a link to a list of acronyms and emoticons and offer to answer any questions until they get the hang of it. If you see that someone has posted something inappropriate, let them know privately. Never do anything to embarrass anyone you know online publicly.

- **Alcohol:** Alcohol and social media don't mix well. Avoid publishing pictures or status updates while under the influence of alcohol, drugs, or strong emotions such as anger or stress. It is better to avoid social media altogether than to regret publishing something embarrassing or potentially damaging to your career. Remember, once it's out there and people have seen it, there's no way to undo it. Try not to appear in pictures if you're drunk; you never know who could see this picture. Publishing this content won't seem like such a good idea the next day.

- **Pictures:** For social gatherings, it is better to take pictures in the early stages of the party where everybody looks good. Always pick the picture in which everyone looks good; they'll thank you for that. Before publishing any picture, you should ask the other people if it's okay to do so and if they approve the picture. It's not very nice to publish a picture in which your friend looks anything short of decent, even if you look totally stunning! It's not the right thing to do, and if you must publish that picture just crop your friend, I'm sure they will appreciate it.

- **Status updates:** You must know your audience; sometimes, you might think it is cool to post something when in reality it just isn't, and your friends might react negatively. If you're unsure about whether to post it or not, it's probably better off the internet.

- **Funny posts:** We all have that one friend who loves to tag us in politically incorrect posts. I won't say I don't enjoy these posts because they never fail to make me laugh. Still, it's a smarter technique to have your friend send them over WhatsApp rather than showing the whole Facebook community as this might backfire and could be offensive or embarrassing to your family members.

Listen Carefully to Your Interlocutor and Look Them in the Eyes As They Talks to You

Showing attention to people is the best way to make them feel comfortable in our presence. Leave your cell phone alone when you are in the company of people. Your concentration must be on the people who are in front of you at that moment. Your friends on Facebook and your followers on Instagram can wait.

Speaker Phone

Do you work in a shared workspace or a cubicle, close enough to coworkers that you can hold conversations without even leaving your seat?

In configurations like these, consider your coworkers when taking phone calls at your desk. If it is not a conference call, don't force them to listen by using the speakerphone. Even if the call is brief, listening aloud is a huge distraction that can affect productivity for everyone around. Sure, you may have no problem tuning out all of the noise around you, but everyone does not share your gift of concentration. If you can avoid unnecessary sounds (especially when it is as simple as picking up the phone), I am certain your coworkers would appreciate you doing so.

Taking Personal Calls

Don't bring them to work if you have had regular, heated arguments with your significant other. If you feel it is too urgent to wait until after work hours, step away from your desk and try to take the call from your car or outside of the building. When you are upset, your voice carries. Even if you think you're speaking in an adequately hushed tone, your coworkers may disagree.

If you are fortunate enough to have an enclosed office instead of a cubicle, you may think you are safe. Think again. Most offices have very thin walls, and even if your colleagues can't hear the words coming out of your mouth, they can likely see your signs of distress through a glass door or window. If you can listen to laughter or chatter outside from time to time, indeed, they can hear you, too.

Maybe your girlfriend is talking down to you out of anger. Or your husband is shouting about an issue you thought was already resolved. In the heat of the moment, you may shout back. Having tense personal conversations at work invites others to form opinions about you unrelated to your job performance. You could come across as a pushover, a bully, or even worse, someone who cannot compartmentalize private issues with work priorities.

The reasons or causes for these arguments are beside the point. You simply do not need your office mates overhearing you discuss various personal matters.

Cell Phone Ringers and Alerts

If you carry a personal cell phone to work, be mindful of the ringer volume. If you wear your phone in a pocket or on a holster, the best solution would be to set your phone to vibrate in the workplace. However, if you must have a ringer turned on for some reason, choose an appropriate ringtone. I recommend a tone at a low volume that sounds similar to an office phone.

Try to refrain from using ringtones of your favorite songs, striking bells, or alarm sounds. Notifications for photos, text messages, and emails also apply. If you get frequent messages throughout the day, just play it safe and keep your device on vibrate. There is nothing more irritating than to hear a coworker's cell phone ringing or alarm going off at their desk while they are nowhere to be found.

If a call comes in that you do not want to accept, do not continue to let the phone ring. If possible, hit ignore on your phone to prevent it from continuing to ring. Also, when your cell phone is set to vibrate, keep it from sitting directly on metal cabinets. Vibrating on metal and other similar surfaces can be just as loud and disruptive as any ringtone! Whatever the case, be mindful of your phone's sound.

Speak Nicely and Do Not Use Swear Words or Offensive Terms

Whichever person you're talking to, don't use bad language. If you have the habit of saying bad words and sometimes you don't even realize it, you can ask those around you to recover every time you say a bad word; little by little, you will relieve yourself of this bad habit. The bad habits you have at home will also take you out. This is true for many things. When we leave the house, we think that we will instantly change our ways, but in reality, nothing is very easy to bring out the bad habits, so try to eliminate them.

There's really no way to integrate into society without communicating. Whether you communicate face-to-face, send notes and stationery, or engage socially through more modern means, such as text message or email. There are numerous ways to do it effectively and properly. Many people struggle with communication in personal interaction—small talk or socializing at events.

As a society, we need to communicate. It's the only way to pass information between one another to achieve goals and activities, in addition to warning each other about danger or the teaching and passing of knowledge. Connections are also made through communication. Think about the last time you had a conversation with someone and learned that you both loved the same book or television show. It bonded you and created the first signs of a foundation in friendship.

Tone

Much like body language, the tone is important in conversation—especially small talk. Some say that the tone of your voice adds more to the conversation than the words! While you might be more aware of how your tone comes across in a face-to-face conversation, it's something to be aware of when talking on the phone. Try this exercise: While smiling, say the phrase 'how are you doing today' and then try it again, this time without smiling. Could you detect a drastic difference in the tone of your words? Aside from the physical changes—which are important when communicating in person—your tone can be changed without you even realizing it.

Word Choice

One common culprit of conversation has too many verbal tics that diminish the quality of the communication. Saying 'umm,' 'like' and other frequently overused terms should be cut out of your vocabulary. First, it's a good idea to know when you say them and make a conscious effort to slow down your speech so that you have time to think about what you want to say rather than fill it with dead words.

Navigating Small Talk

Being in an unknown social setting is stressful enough, but what happens when you need to engage with others rather than stand alone in that dark corner of the room? While you might naturally be outgoing and can strike up a conversation no matter where you are, most people find it difficult to approach a stranger and suddenly find things to say.

Before you step foot in a social event, it's a good idea to understand the foundations of conversation—by understanding certain facets of the situation; you can be armed with knowledge and take some of the stress out of the small talk. Instead of putting so much pressure on yourself to figure out what to talk about, it's a good idea to approach a small conversation much like you would with someone you know.

For example, think about when you talk to a partner or friend. One of you says something, and the other responds or adds something more to the conversation, allowing you to provide more input or take the conversation in new directions. More often than not, you're engaging in small talk with your friends and family—so what makes it so stressful when you're talking to strangers? Of course, there's a level of comfort and familiarity that you're used to when talking to friends that you don't have when you begin a conversation with someone you know.

So what are some things you can do to make small talk a little less painful? Let's go over some of the basics:

Do Not Make Absurd Monologues

I bet you know a talkative person. Here make sure you are not that person for others. Breathe from time to time between speeches and leave space for others to express themselves and participate in the conversation.

While engaged in a conversation with one person, don't ignore either party if another approaches you. Instead, introduce the new arrival to the person you were conversing with. Don't just introduce using the names and stop. Give a little tidbit of information, maybe the person's designation or the nature of your acquaintance (friend, peer, client, departmental opposite number, and so on).

Say No

Politeness isn't passivity or becoming a doormat. Say no when you need to; just do it politely. If someone offers you a drink or smokes and you don't want to imbibe or aren't a smoker, a simple 'No, thank you', or something along those lines is enough. Don't give in if you don't want to. You are not a doormat. Ladies, good manners don't mean that you have to put up with boorish or aggressive behavior from men. If you need to stand up to him, do so. Make sure you can call for help. One of the signs of good breeding was always the ability to hold a conversation. While the breeding part is no longer relevant, a true gentleman or lady can converse on most topics intelligently. Keep yourself informed of what goes on in the world around you. Education, of course, is key to this. Slouching looks shabby—no 2 ways about that. Sit or stand up straight. You look confident, and improving your posture means a stronger back and core.

Remember that manners are based upon kindness, consideration, and respect. Knowing which spoon to eat with is useless if you are doing it to show someone down.

Body Language

You can tell a lot about the conversation based on body language. Is the person you're speaking to giving you undivided attention? Are they distracted and not making eye contact with you? Are they smiling or not? These are all cues you can use to determine how to navigate small talk.

Introverted individuals or those who aren't as socially outgoing as others find it difficult to maintain eye contact for a long time. You don't need to engage in a staring contest with someone to have effective communication, but you should make it a point to have eye contact every so often. One good way of taking the pressure off of communication is to mirror what the other person is doing. Do they make eye contact and then look away for a few moments? You could do the same.

Smiling is another part of body language that plays a major role in small talk. No one really wants to approach someone with a scowl on their face, so it's also something to keep in mind when you're in a social setting. Friendly, relaxed body language makes it easier for those to approach you and viceversa. Body language also depends on gender. In most cases, women are okay with talking in closer proximity and facing each other. At the same time, men tend to stand in a 'V' shape that allows them to make occasional eye contact without giving the appearance of being confrontational.

Read

The refined women are passionate readers. Nothing improves a person's language like reading, plus the more you read, the more you learn, and educated women know how to defend themselves on many topics thanks to their culture. The more different books you read, the more your mind will open, and you will be able to talk confidently with many different people. Study something to improve every day, make yourself more interesting. The classy woman is intelligent and well-trained. With the positive energy of gratitude, we dare to reach out, see, and envision! With the *energizing courage* that springs from our *attitude of gratitude,* we can hear ourselves saying "Oh, yes! Thank you!" to both positive options and necessary challenges.

Our daily education opportunities are huge reasons for thankfulness. We treasure the abilities to read and write, count and figure, and gain practical knowledge for our lives. We find education both in school and out, formally and casually. No matter how and where we learn, we express gratitude for the many goods and generous people who come into our life, staying for a while or for a long time, teaching us treasured lessons and life skills. We find that with this *attitude of gratitude*, we are spurred by curiosity and the love of learning to dig deeper, to seek wider in our quests for knowledge and understanding!

We realize that we value excellence in our education and in those who help us and inform us. With gratitude, education in all of the formal and informal ways it's available to us and the intellectual and practical skills we gain become alive, vital, energized!

With gratitude, there are no limits to what we can learn, what we can achieve! We find ways to learn and do what we need and want with a grateful heart—and gratitude is the key to opening doors for us!

We Take Nothing for Granted

Many people right around us have gone through extreme challenges and still find small and large things for which to be grateful. These people shine for us as examples of living a life of gratitude with all its transforming and reviving aspects!

Gratitude Puts the Rough Stuff and the Small Stuff in Perspective!

More often than we'd like, it's the little daily irritations that throw us off-kilter; however, that takes us out of graciousness and into anger and ugliness. It doesn't have to be that way. We don't have to react badly to small inconveniences or disappointments!

Most of us have been around a few sincere people—and constantly—*positive,* who seem able to keep nearly every incident in a perspective of equilibrium, and who don't "sweat the small stuff." They seem to know that when it comes to the daily irritations and minor challenges of Life, as someone once said (or maybe it's just a bumper sticker that rings true), "It's nearly all *small stuff*"! People who seem to take Life's "oops!" in stride can be a pleasure to be around.

Our *gratitude attitude helps us* be positive and discerning—and more likely to keep things in perspective as we sort out the rough stuff from the small stuff in life—finding good, constructive ways to handle it all!

Don't Make Dramas and Scenes

The elegant woman does not make a bad show of herself either in public or at home. She learns to control her emotions and reactions. In a perfect world, everyone would behave beautifully when they're going about their business, but in reality, the perfect world exists only in a dream. The chances are that on any given day, you're going to see people displaying bad manners in public. Sometimes it will behoove you to say something; other times, you're just going to have to deal with the fact that not everyone is as well behaved as you are.

Back in elementary school, you and your friends probably handled cutting in line in a very efficient fashion: when someone tried to sneak in the line, everyone yelled, "No cut-ins," and the person would sneak to the back of the line. While the no sneaking rule applies in the grown-up world, not everyone abides by it.

If you happen to see someone cutting in front of you in lines, such as at the movies or the register in a store, you can say, "Excuse me, but I was ahead of you." Usually, most people will tell you that they weren't paying attention, they're sorry for cutting in front of you, and they'll move to the end of the line. However, what do you do if the person shrugs and says, "So what are you going to do about it?" In that instance, he's just threatened you, and there's no need to push the point. Manners are all good and fine, but you should never risk your safety and well-being by trying to one-up someone on politeness.

What Do I Do If I See Someone Littering?

If the litter isn't too dirty, you can subtly make your point by picking it up, handing it to the person, and saying, "Excuse me, but you dropped this." Otherwise, you can watch silently as that person displays bad behavior and swear that you'll never duplicate it.

The average organization consists of multiple departments and staff members, all performing a range of different activities to fulfill the organization's business goals. Effective methods of communication enable these individual components to work as a unit. In other words, communication facilitates the success of the organization.

Successful communication involves both expressing and receiving information. You can think of this as input and output. Input comes in the form of messages you receive and then interpret, whereas the output is what you express to others. For a transfer of meaning to succeed, the people communicating have to share certain communication norms or standards. This is where communication etiquette comes in. It refers to the basic rules that govern communication and people's expectations surrounding it.

For example, it determines what people generally find polite and how they expect to be addressed. It also affects the ways they expect information to be presented and how they interpret this information.

CHAPTER 9:

Behavior Etiquette

Meetings

For the most part, a gathering may be the setting or the earth where the elements of expert etiquette will merge. While the person may not yet be prepared for you because they may be planning for the conference or accomplishing something else, one must never appear over 5 minutes right on time to a meeting. As this is often considered irritating and crude, one must early at a gathering. That is also viewed as inconsiderate because it leaves the other individuals involved for you to appear sitting tight, which means an absence of affection for different individuals' opportunities. If one must leave the conference rashly, it's ideal to disclose why you've to leave, to make sure that everybody comprehends why the cause of one warrants the need to leave the meeting early. Introducing people is an art and a means of ensuring good manners and a matter of etiquette. Mistakes made when introducing people can hurt your credibility as a professional and create discomfort and even upsets.

Yet a good introduction can get people off to a great conversational start and build up your credibility as a resourceful and good person to know.

When introducing people to each other, the first pronounced name will be the most respected person.

Do Not Be Jealous or Envious

Classy women never show envy or jealousy because they know their worth and therefore are aware that they are not competing with any woman. If a man decides to go after another woman, they simply let him go and think:" one like this is better to lose than to find". The classy woman is not envious if a woman has a car or a job that is more beautiful than her, rather they are happy for them, and they know that the universe is abundant with everyone; they use the successes of other women inspiration.

Unless you are very wealthy, you may find that you have to share your living quarters with another person at some time in your life, *i.e.,* a flatmate. Having to share a home with another person can turn out to be either a great experience or a complete nightmare. The key to having an extraordinary experience is to establish ground rules from the start. Sharing a flat or house with someone means that there will be little privacy, except in your bedroom or the bathroom. You need to agree on boundaries.

Certain key areas should be clarified:

- **Friends:** You need to discuss friends staying over or spending the weekend, *etc.* When someone starts to spend more than the occasional night, they are living on the property. It also means that the person is sharing electricity, food, water, the bathroom, *etc.*
- **Clothes and belongings:** Establish that there should be no sharing or taking of personal belongings without express permission.
- **Food:** Agree on how groceries should be shared, who cooks, and when. If you cook, it is polite to offer your flatmate(s) some.
- **Cleaning:** It is best to have a turn for cleaning the flat or house and make sure the chores are shared out equally. If you can afford it, get a cleaner.
- **Bills:** Discuss how the bills will be divided and ensure that each person pays their fair share.

Try to discuss all possibilities, e.g., about having parties, who will take out the garbage and when, whether it is acceptable to smoke in the home, etc. The bottom line is, make an effort to get along with your flatmate(s), as this can be a wonderful experience.

Friends

Friends are an essential part of a person's life. It is important to be a good friend and to have good friends. Your friends will enrich your life and will be part of it as you grow, at school, university, throughout your career, in business, and family life. Being a good friend and having good friends takes a lot of effort and patience; consider it a life-long investment. Like anything else in life, there is an element of risk involved. The key qualities that are important for being a good friend are:

- Loyalty.
- Trust.
- Unconditional love.

Being able to share grief and sorrow: Be there for your friends and be a shoulder they can cry on.

- **Generosity:** Give them gifts to show you have thought about them. If you cannot afford gifts, give them your time.
- **Pure acceptance:** Accept them for who they are and do not judge them.
- **Laughter:** Learn to laugh with your friends.

Respect the Law

An elegant woman does not have to appear in the newspaper due to law and police problems.

Visit any big city, and you are bound to see beggars and panhandlers out on the street corner. You should not feel bad about ignoring the people who come at you with an outstretched hand. In addition, you shouldn't feel bad about saying, "No, sorry," when they ask you if you can spare any change, and you don't want to give them anything.

While it's normal to feel sorry for beggars on the street, if you really want to make a difference, you should probably take any money you might give to them and donate it to a nonprofit organization that works with the homeless instead.

You would also be wise to ignore bigots who start spewing racist, hateful things. Unfortunately, people like this tend to be very close-minded individuals. Don't waste your breath trying to argue with them or helping them to see the light of tolerance—it will likely be an exercise in futility. However, if you're fed up listening to them talk, it wouldn't be rude to say, "I don't want to hear this anymore," and to walk away.

The one excessive talker you don't want to ignore is the insensitive jerk who insists on talking during a movie. Many people are indeed used to talking while watching movies at home, but that doesn't give them carte blanche to add a running commentary to a movie that hundreds of others are trying to watch. If the guilty talking party happens to be sitting behind you, you can usually nip the talking problem in the bud by turning around and glaring at the person. A couple of loud "Shhs" goes a long way, too. If it works, you may want to move to another seat or get the theater management involved in shutting the offender up.

Now, what do you do if the talking that's bothering you happens to be coming through the telephone, in the form of a telemarketer? For starters, the "Do Not Call" lists that went into effect recently should have helped to cut down on unsolicited calls—that is, if you signed up. If you didn't, then don't just hang up when you get a call. Tell the person on the line, "Take me off your list." By law, the telemarketer must respect your request, or he risks being fined by the federal government. You need to be patient, though, as it can take months for your number actually to be taken off of these call lists. In the meantime, make "take me off your list" your mantra when dealing with telemarketers. Don't get indignant with telemarketing calls you get from the companies you already do business with. The telemarketer is just trying to do her job, but as an existing customer, you're fair game.

Respect the Queue

Don't try to get smart by running ahead of others in the queue. Your time is worth no more than theirs.

The sign in the supermarket checkout line clearly says, "Ten items or fewer," but you notice that the person in front of you easily has twenty items. What do you do? First, don't take it on yourself to point out this discrepancy. It's the cashier's problem. Second, if you're in a hurry, don't stand there, huff, and puff while the other person checks out. If you need to get somewhere fast, go to another checkout line.

Finally, make sure that you never ever end up in an express line with more items than is allowed. Always do a quick count of your cart before you choose your checkout line, and that way, you'll never be one of those supermarket hogs that everyone hates.

Do Not Disturb

Don't be one of those people who talk on the phone or converse loudly with their friends at the cinema or theater or in the church.

Two surefire ways annoy your neighbors with noise that goes beyond blaring music at all hours of the night. (That's a given.) The first is to install a car alarm that goes off with the slightest vibration. If you must have a car alarm, then at least make sure that it's designed to go off when someone is actually trying to steal your car, not closing a car door next to you.

Some municipalities have passed laws that ban leaf blowers during certain hours or altogether. If you live in one of these places, be careful how you clean up your lawn clippings or autumn leaves. If you take the easy way out with a leaf blower, you may not only be considered rude, but you could also be breaking the law.

The second is to do yard work early on a weekend morning—and with a leaf blower, no less. This nifty cleaning-up tool may save you from sweeping your sidewalks, but in the process, you're probably alienating everyone around you, thanks to the tool's deafening sound.

Be More Feminine

Up until present times, the style of women in western states has evolved. Initially, women were only preoccupied with properly dressing when they had guests coming over, when going out for a social dinner or when invited to a ball. Today much has changed since they began to occupy the highest dignities in the state. For example, Margaret Thatcher, the first female prime minister in Europe, had an elaborate but sober style that emphasized her feminism and power.

Many countries, places, and institutions have their dress code. Although the general rule of thumb is that for certainty, you should always ask what the dress code is, let's review then some of the rules that can help guide any woman to attempt to follow protocol and etiquette. The feminine outfit adopted during the day should define your style, but at the same time be relaxed, elegant, and sober, especially when you hold an essential function within the institution or company.

For the vast majority of diplomats and the vast majority of those working in public functions or companies, the daily choice should consist of a business suit or a classic outfit like a skirt and blazer or a dress.

At the same time, it should be kept in mind that casual never means jeans or shorts. Unlike the United States, most countries do not define casual as jeans and sneakers or sportswear.

Even when it comes to the United States, my recommendation would be that unless it is a strict business meeting or part of a larger conference where the organizers specifically mentioned that the dress code is business, you should wear business attire. In particular, if officials are also present.

For those of you who have business relations with foreign partners, you should know that the rigors vary from country to country and depending on the event that you attend. In particular, women need to be very careful about conservative clothing rules, such as skirt length or neckline depth.

Discourteous Comments

When it comes to discourteous comments, probably the best way to sum things up is to borrow from Britney Spears and say, "Oops, I did it again." Sometimes you just can't help yourself, and you let something slip. Then, after it's out there, you wish you could take it back.

You should develop what some people call an edit function, which is like the 5-second delay in live television. You need to stop and think about what you're about to say before you say it. That way, if it is inappropriate, you can shut your mouth before it's too late. There are many instances in life when an edit function would come in handy, including the following.

Backhanded Compliments

There are times when you may notice that someone you know seems to have changed their look. Maybe she's lost weight or colored her hair, or maybe he's shaved off his facial hair. While people always appreciate hearing compliments about their appearance, you've got to be careful about how you compliment them, lest you insult them in the process.

For example, if you notice that someone has lost weight, don't say, "Holy cow, you used to be such a porker!" Instead, you can gracefully broach the subject of someone's weight loss by saying, "Pardon my asking, but is there less of you now than there was before?"

If you notice other personal changes about a person, again proceed with any compliments carefully. Pointing out that someone has gotten her eyes done may not be a good idea, especially if she's self-conscious about having had cosmetic surgery. However, a good catchall way to raise the topic of someone's changed physical appearance would be to say, "I just can't put my finger on it, but something about you is different, and you look wonderful." Again, this allows you to pay someone a compliment without blatantly pointing out that she really didn't look that great before she made whatever change in appearance it was that you noticed.

Age-Related Questions

Unless you work in a bar or liquor store, you probably shouldn't come out and ask someone their age. This is especially true of women who may be sensitive about aging and are apt to celebrate multiple twenty-ninth birthdays. At the same time, you never want to ask someone his age in a job interview, or you risk setting yourself up for an age-discrimination accusation.

There are times when you may be discussing trivia or pop culture, and you're curious to establish how old the person you're talking to really is. You can get to that information in a roundabout and perfectly polite way. Instead of asking, "How old are you?" you could say, "I hope you don't mind my asking, but what year did you graduate from high school?" This will help place this person on a timeline, and you won't have asked them to reveal their real age. It's clever and courteous.

Braggers

Everyone has something to brag about at one time or another, and usually good friends and family members are happy to hear about your good fortune. It's when you never stop talking about yourself and your good fortune that you risk turning people off. If you find yourself cornered at a cocktail party or in a conversation with a braggart, the most polite and effective way to deal with that person is not to respond to their outrageous claims at all. Silence is an amazing way to humble people. If that doesn't work, you can always try to change the topic. However, if this braggart is like most, they will eventually find a way to bring the conversation back to being all about them. At that point, you can politely excuse yourself and walk away.

Delicately Dealing With Disabilities

If your children happen to see someone who is disabled, they're probably going to ask you about it—usually in a loud enough voice that the person they're asking about can hear them. Sometimes, your children can get a good lesson in tolerance from the person with the disability himself, who may answer their questions for you. Otherwise, it's up to you to handle their questions as matter-of-factly as possible.

When a child asks why someone is sitting in a wheelchair, say, "That person's legs probably don't work as well as yours and mine, and he needs that wheelchair to get around." A simple, straightforward answer should help satisfy their curiosity and teach them a little something about people's differences.

Never scold your child for noticing someone with a disability and asking about them. They are just being curious, and it's your job as a parent to educate them on people's differences.

The other kind of disability that you may have to deal with delicately is when someone doesn't speak as clearly as everyone else because he's had a stroke or stutters. Again, deal with the matter directly if you're with your child, and he asks why someone is speaking oddly. Tell your child that sometimes people are born a certain way and can't talk as well as they'd like to, or they get sick later in life, which affects their speech.

Besides being upfront and honest with your child, you need to be polite to the person by listening closely to what they have to say and being patient while they finish their thoughts. Never assume the part of translator and finish this person's sentence for them. They have likely had years of practice communicating with others, and with a little patience, they will surely get their idea across.

Learn to Greet the Right Way When You Meet Someone

Do not squeeze your hand too tightly or too weakly, and do not pull it towards you. Sunglasses should be removed when you introduce yourself or greet someone. Remember the names and pronounce them correctly.

The handshake is one of the oldest and most common customs for greeting people in most cultures. We may not realize that when we shake hands with people, the handshake makes an impression. Deals are sealed with a handshake, and wars may be averted with a handshake. We often see presidents and heads of state being photographed whilst shaking hands. This should tell us that handshakes are very important, and yet a lot of us underestimate the importance of this seemingly insignificant act.

However, it is important to note that this may not be the case in some cultures, and it is helpful if one can take time to learn about different ways of greeting in different cultures.

The following tips should be considered:

- Always use your right hand and 'pump' the other person's hand 2 or 3 times before you let it go.
- Make sure that your fingers grip the other person's palm; this way, you will not crush their fingers.
- Be careful not to clench the other person's hand in a bone-crushing grip, but do not offer a limp hand.
- Always check that your palms are not sweaty before shaking hands.

Polite and Kindness

The entire journey of sharing and learning with so many wonderful young people, teachers, and parents has been a delight. It's fabulous to be now taking this adventure of meaningful etiquette broader and broader, with opportunities to meet, greet, and interact all along the way!

Some of the *rules* of etiquette seem to make good sense when we think about them; others may seem really weird or seem like they'd make absolutely no difference if we forgot about them! However, many of our etiquette traditions *do* make sense if we use etiquette's so-called *rules*, forms, or guidelines in an instance appropriate for them—and in the particular group for which they were intended!

Etiquette skills are tools, and, just like any other tools we've learned to use, they help us to do things when and how we want them done. Our skillful ability to *do things* opens doors of opportunity and experience—it's simple! Etiquette skills are no exception!

Being able to use our etiquette tools well and appropriately can help us feel confident and feel happier with ourselves. Good etiquette can help us be more comfortable and bring us positive attention—the kind we want! Not having adequate social skills limits us; having them and practicing them makes us ready for opportunities!

Mindful Kindness!

Practicing these etiquette skills brings us more pleasant daily social interactions, increases our self-confidence and helps to open doors of opportunity for ourselves—and graciously holds the doors of opportunity open for others.

Since everyone wants to feel good, no matter the differences in life experiences, opportunities, or traditions, a little or a lot of kindness goes a long way.

Treating Others as We Believe We'd like to Be Treated

In our Etiquette of Kindness endeavors, we always try to consider and respect that there are various ethnic and family traditions.

We realize that:
- Not every social skill we learn is universally accepted or useful.
- Not everyone's experiences in Life are the same as ours.

However, the desire to be treated with kindness *is* common to us all. So, though we can never walk exactly in another person's path, we try to treat others as we would like to be treated—and we are grateful for kindness and consideration being shown to us.

We do our best in a good, positive spirit—and *trust* that others also act from this sort of attitude. We know that we—and others in their turn—will be imperfect in attempts at kindness, but still, we offer kindness and courtesy genuinely, and most often, we find this comes to us as well. However, it's not the *return* that prompts us to be kind: kindness, consideration, gratitude, and courtesy—each is its own reward.

Extending these qualities to others as best we can do and determine not only provides good positive feelings *out there*, but it also automatically makes us happier—more creative, more expansive in our brains, and more peaceful in our hearts and minds. In addition, there's additional good news: as we live more kindly, we realize that it's more fun to act in kindness!

This all adds up to excellent reasons for learning and practicing The Etiquette of Kindness!

It Is Always Good to Be Grateful!

It is *always* correct, needed, and basic to say "thank you!" when any type of kindness, consideration, or generosity—and to mean it! We say "thank you!" when we are given:

- Small gestures of courtesy in any day-to-day setting.
- Gifts of time, thoughtfulness, generosity, sharing—all of which should be acknowledged at the moment.
- Larger gestures of kindness that deserve not only a "Thank you so much!" at the moment, but *also* a more formal "thank you again!" for any physical gift given or for any notable act of kindness, generosity, and thoughtfulness.
- These words of gracious gratitude are universal in their preference, appreciation, and appropriateness; their use has no age or gender limitation!

Often, a simple gesture of courtesy given to us makes us more aware of being courteous ourselves, and we are prompted to pass along an act of thoughtfulness to others. From one thoughtful, courteous person to another, kindness grows!
Daily, we find opportunities to offer kindly acts such as:

- Opening or holding a door for another person.
- Helping someone on/off with their coat or jacket.
- Assisting in carrying items or relieving another of a heavy burden.

- Getting up in open seating (waiting area, train, or bus) to offer another person our seat.
- Offering a place to sit to a person who may be considerably older, apparently unsteady in posture, or heavily burdened—or to someone who is *just another human being*. We are inclined to be generous and helpful.
- Sliding in to allow others to be seated easily in a non-assigned row or, at the very least, rising or adjusting in our seat to ease others in being seated.
- Offering a hand to a person who might need assistance in getting in or out of a car, or maybe in crossing a stream of water.
- Offering another person to step in front of us at the grocery line when we are heavily laden with purchases.

Now, we understand that some people, sometimes, may not welcome our offer of help or assistance. In fact, our perceptions of what is *helpful* might be very different from another's, and our offer might even be considered offensive or insulting! We may find ourselves surprised by an occasional verbal reprimand for our having offered aid.

In all cases, we are courteous ourselves in our response! Whether the other person refuses our offer graciously or not, we don't waiver from being respectful. We don't press what we think should be considered *courteous* and accepted by the other person or what we want in a situation. We respect the other person's thoughts, stances, and sensitivities—and we graciously go on with whatever we are doing.

Doing Our Best Because We Care!

We try to show kindness and consideration in everything we do thoughtfully. We do the best that we can determine—and we go from there, always developing and always grateful for our *Etiquette of Kindness* skills!

It's Not Just About You

An organization's image is at just as much risk as an individual's. Companies have to worry about negative publicity in newspapers, radio, television, and the Internet.

You should try to maintain an image of professionalism even when you're not in the office. To do this, you should remove any potentially compromising material from the Internet, refrain from making negative or disparaging comments, and always maintain a sense of decorum.

Politeness and Cooperation

Relationships are key to business success. Once you've made a positive first impression, you can use business etiquette to help build healthy work relationships. At this stage, it's essential to develop rapport and to behave with trust and integrity.

There are 3 stages of building strong relationships: making a good first impression, following proper etiquette, and managing challenging situations.

Practicing and nurturing your social intelligence can help you do this. Social intelligence refers to how you manage your interactions with other people, how well you get along with them, and how effective you are at getting them to cooperate with you.

People with high social intelligence interact in a way that draws others to them. They make others feel empowered, appreciated, and respected. Conversely, people with low social intelligence interact in ways that drive others away or make them feel intimidated, frustrated, and devalued.

An Attitude of Gratitude!

One of the main ways to bring joy into our lives is to have an *attitude of gratitude*— to daily find and name small and large things for which to be grateful, beginning with our first wakefulness in the morning, then continuing during our day and right on through our last moments before sleep! Whenever we feel lackluster and *bored*, an instant antidote to boredom is to turn our attention to gratitude. Boredom flees in the face of gratitude!

The healing and instant refreshment properties of gratitude can be *magical*, giving new life and *elasticity* to our brains and creating happy moments that build good days. Gratitude is *energizing!*

Our Glass—Half-Empty or Half-Full?

When we are thinking negatively and narrowly—without gratitude—our heart, mind, and body reflect this. In this frame of mind, we can see a simple drinking glass filled halfway, and our perception is that it's half-*empty!*

With a negative attitude, we tend to think with restrictions. In this mindset, "No!" is often our response to ideas, limiting our brain's free exploration of possibilities and creative options! Our hearts are not open to wonderful, positive associations and opportunities when we think, act, and live in negativity and lack. Our body shows negativity as well. It mirrors our sense of dejection and hopelessness in our sour facial expression, hanging head, and shuffling walk. When we think negatively, we also tend to take poor care of ourselves, perhaps eating too little or too much, staying inside in isolation, and avoiding exercise.

However, when we decide to *think and act out of gratitude*, our sense of ourselves, other people, and our experiences changes dramatically to the positive. Even that drinking glass that we formerly considered half-empty becomes for us half-full!

With gratitude, we can think more widely and creatively. As "Yes!" becomes our attitude, options come to us more readily and with a sense of possibility and opportunity! Our associations with people can lighten and improve as our hearts open in gratitude; we find ourselves attracted to other positive, engaged people, and they to us!

Our body reflects our gratitude. We find ourselves smiling, our posture is straighter, and our walk peppier. With gratitude, even our appreciation of Nature is revived, and we may find we *need* to be out-of-doors, getting exercise and breathing fresh air. With an *attitude of gratitude*, we often find that we are simply taking better care of ourselves, getting more rest, and gratefully enjoying a bounty of fresh, healthful foods in appropriate portions for our health.

Whether we consider ourselves an introvert or an extrovert, whether we are quiet and shy or outgoing and brimming with confidence—*gratitude* has the power to make our life far better! And gratitude, it turns out, is the basis for living our lives in the *Etiquette of Kindness*! (Who knew?). Everyone can easily find gratitude for the simplest and the most profound things.

We feel grateful for a drink of water to quench our thirst and for a deep, life-giving breath; for the sun's rising in the morning and for the breezes cooling our face; for the warmth of summer and for the moon's coaxing plants from the soil; for the renewing rain and chilling snow wetting our head and watering the earth.

We can be inspired to gratitude by the scents of roses and jasmine, mint, strawberries, and mangoes, by the intoxicating smells of baking brownies, hot popcorn, brewing coffee, and cinnamon rolls right from the oven. We can realize thankfulness for the happy yelp and tail-wagging greeting of a beloved dog, for the peaceful purr of a contented cat, and for the chirps and trilling of birds on the wing. Gratitude opportunities are everywhere, and we have them in abundance!

Etiquette for Beginners

Conclusion

Thank you for making it through to the end of this book and being willing to learn just some of the ways that you can transform, grow, and strengthen your self-image. However, there is a surprise: the work begins now! This means that the information you have obtained cannot just be stored in your memory bank. It must be used at every possible opportunity at home, school, work, or at play.

An individual prerequisite will never end, so I have attempted to clarify some significant territories where humans get different opportunities to improve a decorum's level to be the best in their general public.

Better communication and shared trust will generate if you feel great around somebody and one other way around. This secure area is identified through introducing yourself. Etiquette gives you some guidance with obtaining this. As you have seen by now, elegance can be a major part of daily life. When you're at the grocery store, and you nearly run into someone with a cart, do you say 'excuse me' as if it's second nature? Do you hold the door open for someone coming in from behind you? When you host a party, do you go out of your way to ensure your guests don't sit in silence at the table, or do you tell your child to mind their manners and chew with their mouth closed?

All of these scenarios are a matter of acting gracefully. While you might know some, hopefully, there have been instances throughout this book where you learned what to say (and what not to say!) to someone going through pregnancy or a death in the family.

Etiquette isn't just something you learn once and then have that knowledge forever—it's constantly changing to accommodate the modern world and all of the updates within it, such as technology!

Now that you've gotten an idea as to just how much etiquette plays a role in our daily lives and with everyone that we come across, we hope you continue learning and understanding the various tips and recommendations for different areas of your life. Whether it's throwing a wedding or baby shower or learning how to tip at restaurants and taking public transportation, how you can grow and be a more graceful and elegant person is endless—which all of us benefit from learning such foundations in etiquette.

Therefore, I trust this book will assist you with improving your habits level in reality. Good luck.

Made in the USA
Middletown, DE
14 April 2022